LEADING GROWTH

DR. EUGENE T. WILSON

WORD AFLAME PRESS
HAZELWOOD, MO

WORD AFLAME PRESS
8855 Dunn Road, Hazelwood, MO 63042
www.pentecostalpublishing.com

© 2016 by Eugene T. Wilson

All rights reserved. No portion of this publication may be reproduced, stored in an electronic system, or transmitted in any form or by any means, electronic, mechanical, photocopy, recording, or otherwise, without the prior permission of Word Aflame Press. Brief quotations may be used in literary reviews.

All Scripture verses quoted are from the New King James Version unless otherwise identified.

New King James Version © 1982 by Thomas Nelson, Inc. Used by permission. All rights reserved.

Printed in the United States of America.

Cover design by Elizabeth Loyd

Library of Congress Cataloging-in-Publication Data

Names: Wilson, Eugene T., author.
Title: Leading growth / Eugene T. Wilson.

Description: [Hazelwood, MO] : Word Aflame Press, [2015] | Includes bibliographical references.

Identifiers: LCCN 2016007550| ISBN 9780757750120 (pbk. : alk. paper) | ISBN 9780757750137 (ebook)

Subjects: LCSH: Christian leadership. | Christian life. | Leadership--Religious aspects--Christianity.

Classification: LCC BV652.1 .W51447 2015 | DDC 253--dc23 LC record available at http://lccn.loc.gov/2016007550

Dedicated to my father, Harrell T. Wilson,
and my son, Eugene Kade Wilson.

One I follow; the other I lead.
Both have blessed my life.

CONTENTS

Acknowledgments 9
Introduction 11
Chapter 1 - OVERCOMING THE OSTRICH EFFECT 15
    Churches are declining 16
    Church attendance is declining 17
    What about large churches? 18
    What about growing churches? 19
    What about church plants? 20
    Are you serious about growth? 21
Chapter 2 - PEOPLE ARE NOT GROWING 23
    Pastors don't think people are growing 24
    Why we should be cautious of the church growth movement 26
    Church growth is not people growth 29
    Keeping the horse before the cart 30
Chapter 3 - WHY DO YOU WANT TO GROW? 33
    Ask "Why?" again and again 34
    Who am I trying to impress 37
    The struggle with ego is real 38
    Criticism and ego 42
    Overcome ego with humility 43
    Conclusion 45
Chapter 4 - ARE YOU ALIGNED WITH GOD'S PLAN? 47
    Jesus and church growth 48
    Paul and church growth 48
    We are called to equip others 50
    Everyone is to be involved in ministry 52
    What do my actions reveal? 53
    Do I want what God wants? 56
Chapter 5 - MEASURING GROWTH 59
    Get rid of the old scoreboard 60
    A new scoreboard 62
    How can we know people are growing? 65
    How can we know that we are developing leaders? 67
    How do we gauge culture? 68
    How healthy is your practice of culture and team building? 70
    Conclusion 72

Chapter 6 - LEADERSHIP STYLES 73
   A leader of growth 73
   Do you "get" it? 75
   Leadership defined 76
   Styles of leadership 77
   Purposeful leadership 80
   Conclusion 83

Chapter 7 - WHAT'S ALL THE HOOPLA ABOUT SERVANT LEADERSHIP? 85
   Servant leadership 87
   Why you should want to be a servant leader 88
   The tension in servant leadership 90
   Reconciling leadership and servanthood 92
   Transformational leadership 95
   Conclusion 96

Chapter 8 - GROWTH ACTIVITIES 99
   What high-performing executives do 99
   What Jesus did 101
   Simple things leaders of growth do 103
   Conclusion 112

Chapter 9 - IS ACCOUNTABILITY EFFECTIVE? 115
   Good and bad accountability 116
   Why hold people accountable? 117
   Philosophy impacts accountability 120

Chapter 10 - STRATEGIC THINKING FOR GROWTH 123
   Five growth principles 124
   Strategy 126
   Strategy and discipleship 127
   Strategy and leadership development 129
   Strategy and vision 132
   Strategy and structure 133
   Strategy and strategic thinking 135
   Conclusion 139

Chapter 11 - GROW YOURSELF 141
   How to become a healthy leader 146
   The greatest enemy of personal growth 155
   Epilogue 157
   Conclusion 159

Bibliography 161
Endnotes 169

ACKNOWLEDGEMENTS

A book has never been written nor a life lived that has not been influenced by others. The same is true with this book as well as the life of its author.

I owe a great debt to those who have helped to shape my life—many with whom I share a close relationship, and some whom I admire from afar. You have taught me faithfulness, to enjoy the journey, to pursue peace, to let bygones be bygones, to love, to hope, and to trust. You have helped me grow. For this, I am forever grateful.

INTRODUCTION

JUST A FEW YEARS REMOVED from a Bible college, I was asked to speak at a youth event. After introducing me, the pastor exited the platform to sit on the front pew. (This was during a time when pastors almost always sat on the platform.) I noticed several times as I was preaching the pastor stood and clapped his hands in support, as did others throughout the congregation. Things were going well, at least for the moment.

Then something happened. It surprised me. I declared, "God wants this church to grow!" But instead of a resounding "amen," or a show of support with the clapping of hands, there was nothing. The silence was deafening. I was stunned. What had I done?

I continued ministering but my words appeared to have little effect. The damage had been done. There was nothing I could do. Afterward, the pastor and members of the congregation were kind, yet little was said, and I went my way.

Sometime later I discovered the reason for the lack of response. Not long before I arrived, the pastor had told the congregation they did not need to grow. He'd said large churches meant more problems, and they did not need more problems.

How can someone not desire growth, even though problems may increase? There are so many people who need God, so many who need His help. What was the pastor thinking?

Sadly, I have come to learn of others who have little desire for growth. Few of them have been as brash as the pastor I encountered as a young minister. But they exist nonetheless. Such church leaders resist change, even when it is in their best interest to do so: they refrain from seeking an accurate assessment of leadership skills; they function with erroneous concepts of pastoral responsibility and authority; they are most interested in maintaining the status quo; and so on.

But this does not describe most church leaders. Most church leaders want to grow. Most church leaders want to help people to experience growth. And most church leaders want to lead growing churches.

If you want growth—if you are willing to do what is necessary to grow—then this book is for you. My prayer is you will find something amongst these pages that will benefit you in your journey. If, however, you are content with the way things are, if you do not want to deal with the challenges that arise from growth, then you will not get much out of this book. Please put it down. Reading it will be a waste of your time.

You may ask yourself, "What does the author know about growth? Why should I listen to what he has to say? Has he ever led a growing church, or a church of our size?" I admit I do not know all there is to know about growth—I don't believe anyone does. Although I have served as a senior pastor and on pastoral teams in both small churches as well as large churches, I have not experienced every aspect of church growth. Again, I don't believe anyone has.

Most professional golfers have a coach; only a few do not. Tiger Woods, one of the greatest golfers to ever play the game, has had a golf coach for most of his career. Golf coaches do not play the PGA, but that does not make them any less effective as a coach. A good coach can look at a player's swing, see what the golfer needs to do differently, and instruct the golfer how to correct his swing. Amazingly, golf players are so close to the subject matter they cannot see what is obvious to the trained eye of the coach.

Similarly, no one in his right mind would make it a prerequisite that his doctor must have the same disease he has in order for the doctor to help him. That would be ludicrous. Doctors spend years in training, years in observation, and years in helping people with diseases. They are qualified to help others. Doctors are not required to have the same disease in order to be effective; doctors are required to have training in how to help people with the disease.

Hence, openness is the first key to growth. Leaders who do not open themselves to receive will not receive. Thus a leader of growth does not shun words of instruction, even if they were to come from a donkey. You never know who or what God might use to speak to you.

So open yourself. Allow yourself to be challenged. Ultimately, the decision to grow or not to grow is yours. Yes, contrary to the opinion of some, you get to decide. Growth is not left to chance. Anyone can experience it. But, in the words of Allen Oggs, "You gotta have the want to."

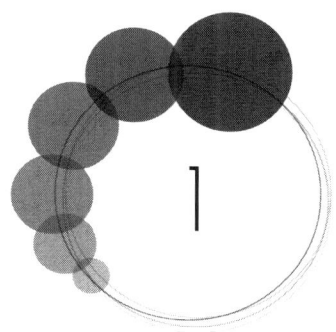

1

OVERCOMING THE
OSTRICH EFFECT

IT HAS LONG BEEN BELIEVED that ostriches bury their heads in sand when feeling scared or threatened. Because they cannot see the danger, they feel safe even though the situation may be dire.

The ostrich effect describes people who are in denial of a situation or refuse to acknowledge the facts. It describes people who by choice fail to see what is plainly before them.

Why would anyone discard the facts? Why would anyone choose to ignore what is before them? One reason is that facts often paint a negative picture. While there is value in limiting one's exposure to negativity, an accurate assessment of a situation is not necessarily negative, no matter how bleak it may be. In fact, embracing the truth of a situation can prove beneficial. Once reality is embraced one can then see what must change.

Leaders are often tempted to deny reality as though the acceptance of reality is an acceptance of defeat. But this is not true. This is faulty thinking. The acceptance of reality is the first step in identifying what must not be allowed to remain the same. Moreover, the denial of facts or truth does not change reality. Instead, it lessens the likelihood of movement toward a desired future.

Thus, positive movement must involve the facts. Nehemiah is a perfect example. Nehemiah embraced reality. The walls of Jerusalem were in ruins; something had to be done. The rebuilding of the walls began with an acceptance of reality. Before Nehemiah could take appropriate action, he first had to come to terms with the reality of the situation (Nehemiah 2:11–15).

The prodigal son is another example. The prodigal came to himself (Luke 15:11–32). In order for the prodigal son to create a better future for himself, he had to come to terms with the reality of his situation. It was this acceptance of reality that enabled the prodigal to recognize his need for change; it also created willingness within to do something about it.

I believe it is possible to look at facts (even those of a negative connotation) and take positive action. In fact, I believe it is essential to forward movement. Sadly, many leaders resist such action. But leaders who experience forward movement do not.

We begin by looking at the current state of North American churches, dismal though it may be. We do so, however, with the hope that it will ignite within church leaders a willingness to do what is necessary to change things for the better.

CHURCHES ARE DECLINING

Unfortunately, most churches are not growing. Church researcher and author George Barna, in *Marketing the Church*, remarks,

> *Since 1980, there has been no growth in the proportion of the adult population that can be classified as "born again" Christian. The proportion of born again Christians has remained constant at 32 percent, despite the fact that churches and para-church*

organizations have spent billions of dollars on evangelism. More than 10,000 hours of evangelistic television programming have been broadcast, in excess of 5,000 new Christian books have been published, and more than 1,000 radio stations carry Christian programming. Yet despite such widespread opportunities for exposure to the Gospel, there has been no discernible growth in the size of the Christian body.[1]

Barna wrote this in 1990. Today things are no better and in many ways have gotten worse. Virtually every mainline denomination, except for a couple of Pentecostal denominations and the Mormons, is experiencing decline.[2] This includes denominations such as the Southern Baptist Convention—a conservative evangelical denomination of over sixteen million members, the United Methodist Church, the Evangelical Lutheran Church in America, the Presbyterian Church USA, and the United Church of Christ, all of which are reporting a decrease in membership.[3]

CHURCH ATTENDANCE IS DECLINING

The decline in church membership coincides with a drop in church attendance. In 1998 the median attendance at main worship services was 70; in 2006 the number was 65; and in 2012 the median attendance was 60.[4] Although the decline is small, it is consistent in the direction it is headed—downward.

People don't consider church attendance to be as important as they once did. Church involvement used to be a cornerstone of the American life. Today, however, US adults are virtually evenly divided on its importance, with nearly half saying it is "somewhat" or "very important," while the other half claims it is "not too" or "not at all" important.[5] Furthermore, nearly one-third (29 percent) of US adults seldom or never attend worship services, and just a little over one-third (36 percent) claim to be regular attendees.[6]

As one might expect, as churches decline in attendance, the number of atheists and agnostics increases. Indeed, between 2007 and 2014 the number of atheists and agnostics nearly doubled.[7] Laurie Goodstein, in an article appearing in *New York Times*, states, "Nearly one in five Americans say they are atheist, agnostic or 'nothing in particular.'"[8] She notes, "This is a significant jump from only five years ago, when adults who claimed 'no religion' made up about 15 percent of the population. It is [also] a seismic shift from 40 years ago, when about 7 percent of American adults said they had no religious affiliation."[9]

Interestingly, when the numbers of atheist and agnostics are combined with the number of "nones" (those who claim to have no religious preference), the number is more than the combined membership of Evangelical Lutherans, United Methodists, and Episcopalians.[10]

Unfortunately, it doesn't appear things are going to get better anytime soon, not when looking at what research says concerning Millennials. According to research, "Among Americans ages 18–29, one in four say they are not currently affiliated with any particular religion."[11] Only two in ten believe church attendance is important, and more than one-third of millennial young adults (35 percent) have taken an anti-church stance.[12]

WHAT ABOUT LARGE CHURCHES?

What about megachurches? Does the increase in the number of megachurches suggest things are changing for the better?

It's true—we have more large churches in America than ever. Statistics show in 2012 there were approximately "1,600 Protestant churches in the United States with a weekly attendance of 2,000 people or more," which is "nearly 25 percent more than 2005."[13] But in spite of the increase in the number of large churches, things are not getting better. Daily exposure to ministries like those of Rick Warren, Joel Osteen, T. D. Jakes, and others, through various forms of media such as television, radio, Internet, social media, and so on, is having little effect on the overall health of America's churches. Only 10 percent of churches in America average more than 350 people in attendance, and 50 percent of churches in America average less than 100 people in attendance.[14] All total, 90 percent of churches in America average fewer than 350 people in worship attendance.[15] Thus it would be wrong to believe things are headed in the right direction just because of a few large churches.

WHAT ABOUT GROWING CHURCHES?

What about growing churches? According to research by Faith Communities Today, evangelical churches with more than 1,000 people experienced an 83 percent increase over a five-year period.[16] Does the increase in growing churches indicate things are beginning to turn around? Well, not exactly.

It is understandable how some people, when considering the growth of some churches, may think things are not as bad as they are. After all, the number of large churches is increasing; and large churches are getting larger in size. Furthermore, according to research, the average church attendee attends a growing church. (This is because more people would rather attend a large growing church than a smaller church, even though there are more smaller-size churches than large ones.) Surely, considering the increase that is occurring in large churches, things are not as bad as some project them to be.

Critics of church growth, however, beg to differ. For example, David Dunlap, in "The Myth of 'Growth' in the Church Growth Movement," claims that much of church growth is nothing more than the simple rearranging of saints.[17] According to research, Dunlap is correct.

Research shows that much of church growth comes not from conversions, but rather it is the result of transfers. In fact, research shows that transfers make up to 80 percent of church growth.[18] Dunlap states, "Many evangelicals are merely playing 'musical churches,' moving from smaller traditional churches to larger more 'exciting' churches."[19]

Dunlap does not stand alone in his assertion that church growth is mostly a relocation of church members from smaller churches to larger churches. Jeffery VanGoethem, pastor of Scofield Memorial Church, speaking from personal observation, states,

> *I kept a running list in my previous ministry in Illinois of all the church plants in the city where I lived. In an area of 125,000 people or so, over a fifteen-year period I counted at least 35 church plants. Although a few succeeded in growing a decent sized congregation (most did not), I did not hear of even one of them that was founded primarily on evangelism and new converts. In contrast to this, an interesting thing happened to a friend of mine who pastors in the country of Zimbabwe. He went back home one time to a rural area to preach the funeral of a relative. He gave a gospel message at the service. Between forty and fifty people were saved at that service—and a new church was established on the strength of these conversions.*[20]

Unfortunately, it appears that Dunlap and VanGoethem might be accurate in their assessments. Churches that are built primarily on new conversions are an exception, not the norm.

WHAT ABOUT CHURCH PLANTS?

Some might maintain an increase in church planting is turning things around. But most church plants do not survive. Furthermore, we are not planting enough churches to keep up with the growth of population anyway. David T. Olson, in *The American Church in Crisis*, states, "Approximately 4,000 churches are started annually that survive at least one year. Unfortunately, many are very small, and these 'low birth weight' churches have a high infant mortality rate. To keep up with population growth caused by new Americans, our country needs an additional 2,900 churches started each year."[21]

Thus, at the current rate of growth of population we continue to fall drastically behind.

ARE YOU SERIOUS ABOUT GROWTH?

Clearly, things are headed in the wrong direction. So what is the answer? How do we turn things around?

Those who are serious about growth should pause and consider these questions: Is this the type of growth—building churches by doing things that attract people from other churches—that is needed? If this is what we are learning from leaders of growing churches (how to attract saints from other churches), should we be listening? Is learning methods and practices for attracting members of other churches a New Testament method for church expansion?

Apparently, some think so. Some think we are called to grow churches. And some have learned the art in doing so. Some have learned how to identify a desired target, craft an appealing message designed specifically for that target, create a slick marketing scheme, and boom—a church of hundreds, if not thousands, can be birthed in no time at all.

But serious church growth advocates may want to consider a different alternative. While there certainly are some things that can be learned from megachurches, just because a church is large in number does not mean everyone should mimic what the church is doing.

Please do not misunderstand me. I am not against growing churches, that is, churches that are increasing in size. I am simply illustrating our need for something different—a different way of leading, a different way of doing things, a different focus. I am simply pointing out what appears to be misplaced emphasis. I am trying to call us into alignment with our calling.

Clearly things are not headed in the right direction. Something is amiss. And yet there is hope. This is His church, and He is building it.

Our responsibility is simple. We are to align ourselves with His purpose and plan for fulfilling His purpose.

2

PEOPLE ARE NOT GROWING

THE FACT THAT CHURCHES ARE DECLINING should be a cause for concern. And this concern should cause us to dig deeper, to gain a more robust understanding of what is occurring. That churches are experiencing a decline is only a portion of the story. The dynamics of church, in many ways, are being altered, and not for the better.

George Barna states, "The nature of churchgoing is changing. Regular attenders used to be people who went to church three or more weekends each month—or even several times a week. Now people who show up once every four to six weeks consider themselves regular churchgoers."[1]

Interestingly, this change in the nature of churchgoing is often missed, even in research. According to Barna Group's tracking data, 43 percent claimed to attend church in 2004 and 36 percent today.[2] But a research project conducted by Richard Krejcir found church attendance is likely much worse than what survey results report.[3]

Krejcir states, "When we started to count people from denominational reports and compare to census data and University research data, the numbers that were originally declared dropped by half."[4] The differentiation was due to how the question regarding church attendance was asked. Krejcir says that in his research project he sought frequency over just attending (frequency was deemed as attending church two times a month as opposed to a few times a year).[5]

A Gallup Poll survey, in which interviewers asked respondents questions regarding their churchgoing habits, such as "In the last seven days, did you attend a church service, excluding weddings and funerals?" supports Krejcir's assertions.[6] Gallup Poll Editor in Chief Frank Newport says, "No matter how we ask the question to people, we get roughly 40 percent of Americans who present themselves as regular church attendees."[7] But Newport admits that on any given Sunday morning you will find fewer than 40 percent actually in church. He states, "Although about 40 percent of Americans are regular church attendees, it doesn't necessarily mean 40 percent are in church on any given Sunday. The most regular church attendee gets sick or sleeps in."[8]

Considering these findings, what does this tell us about the health of the congregations that comprise America's churches? What does this tell us about the spiritual health of the people? Are those who claim to be Christians, who claim to be regular churchgoing people, yet show up twice a month or less, healthy and growing? How about those who truly attend regularly—are they growing? Are they involved in meaningful ministry, fulfilling God's plan and purpose for their life? Are churchgoers making disciples of others? These questions and others like them must be asked for an accurate assessment of the overall health of people.

PASTORS DON'T THINK PEOPLE ARE GROWING

The primary reason people attend church is to grow closer to God and to learn more about Him.[9] But the majority of church leaders

PEOPLE ARE NOT GROWING

believe most of the people in their churches are not growing. Surveys indicate church leaders are correct in their assessment. Fewer than two out of ten churchgoers feel close to God, and only 6 percent claim to have learned something about God the last time they attended church.[10] Did you catch that? Only 6 percent claim to have learned about God the last time they attended church! People are not growing.

Consider the following statistics of a research project in which church leaders were asked questions concerning the spiritual growth of people:[11]

- Eighty-three percent said their people were content in their Christian faith.
- Eighty-one percent said there was no primary teaching from the pulpit to challenge or deepen their people's Christian formation at their church.
- Sixty-nine percent said that more than 70 percent of their congregation members do not assess their spiritual journey or have a means to effectively examine their spiritual lives.
- Sixty percent of church leaders said that more than 60 percent of their congregational members do not have an accurate view of biblical truths.
- Sixty percent of the church leaders said that more than 60 percent of their congregational members do not have an accurate view of their personal spiritual growth. They believe they are growing, but put little to no effort into their growth.
- Fifty-six percent of the church leaders said that more than 60 percent of their congregational members consider themselves as conservative Christians but do not practice that in how they talk, behave, or vote in elections.

- Fifty-three percent of the church leaders said that more than 60 percent of their congregational members do not have a daily devotional life nor are they devoted to growing their spiritual lives.

What is the cause for the lack of growth in people? Is there something that church leaders need to do differently? Is there something church leaders or churches need to add to the already extensive lists of things they are already doing?

Some might think the answer is found in implementing the right programs. If we get the right program up and running people will start growing. But programs abound and people are not growing.

So why are so many church leaders investing so much time, energy, and resources in implementing new programs, revising old programs, and chasing after church growth strategies? Why aren't more church leaders asking questions such as, "Should church growth be our primary focus?" Why aren't more church leaders focusing on growing people? Doesn't it make sense that if people grow, the likelihood of the church experiencing growth will increase substantially? Why are so many church leaders constantly working at implementing programs to increase the size of congregations while working so little on the systems and structures that enhance the possibility of growth in people? Why do church leaders routinely make the pursuit of church growth their chief objective?

WHY WE SHOULD BE CAUTIOUS OF THE CHURCH GROWTH MOVEMENT

Perhaps the church growth movement is to blame.

Birthed in the 1970s, the church growth movement has influenced the thoughts and philosophies of many church leaders. During the '70s the primary teachings of the church growth movement centered on getting church leaders to see the need in meeting the sociological and psychological needs of people. During the '80s the focus was on "leadership and growth barriers such as not enough parking lots and inadequate facilities."[12] During the '90s focus shifted to "how we do worship to attract people."[13] And yet there has been no significant change.

There is certainly some validity in addressing parking lot needs, service flow, beautifying our buildings, as well as other things the church growth movement has taught us. But we must remember such things are merely tools. They should not be the primary focus of church leaders. Neither are they the root cause for the decline of churches. While there are some positives of the church growth movement, there are also some negatives. And perhaps the biggest negative is an overemphasis on numbers. Jeffery VanGoethem states, "Some churches are doing a terrific job of gathering in large numbers of worshippers. This is what many people refer to today when they speak of church growth. But as we have seen, much of this is not true church growth from a biblical perspective."[14]

An overemphasis on numbers is not the type of growth that is needed. In 1939, G. Campbell Morgan sounded a warning applicable for today when he wrote, "When a technique is necessary to get people to listen to the gospel there will be failure. That is not the method of Christ."[15]

Unfortunately, this is exactly what many churches are doing. In an attempt to attract a crowd many are focusing on marketing the gospel. While marketing certainly has its place, it should not be the primary focus of church leaders. By marketing, I am not necessarily referring to advertisements; I am referring to the efforts of church leaders to meet the consumer mentality that has crept into churches. Tom Rainer, in "Eleven Observations about Church Transfer Growth," remarks, "Many Christians have become nothing more than church hoppers and shoppers to find the right church that meets their needs and preferences. They view a local congregation as a country club with perks for the members."[16]

Consider what Greg Laurie, senior pastor of Harvest Christian Fellowship in Riverside, California, has to say about the church growth movement. In an article titled "Four Dangerous Church Growth Myths," he cautions against growing churches, that is, focusing on numerical growth and following after some church growth methods and practices.[17] Interestingly, Laurie's church has some fifteen thousand people.

Laurie says he is against growing churches when it involves a willingness to do anything to increase the number of attendees. He claims that justifying the means for the end result can prove harmful to the church body. Laurie states, "What makes a church body grow big doesn't necessarily make it grow healthy."[18]

Some, in an attempt to grow churches, are willing to water down the gospel message so the unbeliever will feel comfortable attending church. Laurie states, "I'm concerned that in a sincere effort to get their churches to grow, some are exchanging entertainment for exhortation and gimmicks for the Gospel."[19] He continues, "Of course, drama, videos, music and other media used to communicate Christian faith in churches today aren't compromises by themselves. Yet we must be sure gimmicks don't take the place of the Gospel."[20] While we should be wise in how we deal with people, we also must not be shy in sharing the truth. What good is it to have a large crowd if the people in the crowd remain unchanged?

Perhaps most surprising, though, is Laurie's viewpoint regarding feeding the felt needs of people, a major aspect of seeker-sensitive churches. Laurie sounds a caution against it: "A church with a steady diet of feel-good sermonettes in place of solid teaching from Scripture might eventually grow to become a large congregation—but it will be weak and immature."[21] And remember, Laurie is the pastor of a church of fifteen thousand members. Don't miss the point: Greg Laurie is not against large churches; he is against focusing on church growth as opposed to the growth of people.

Do Laurie's concerns have merit? It certainly seems so. His remarks are applicable in every church, both large and small churches, both growing and stagnating churches. Watering down the gospel message in an attempt to attract people is wrong. Using gimmicks to grow the church must never outshine the gospel message. And what may make a church body grow (numerically) may be harmful to the health of the church body (people). Such reflection should cause us to ask, "What are we trying to do—grow a church or grow people?"

You may disagree. You may favor the church growth movement and think my assertion has little merit. If so, listen to C. Peter Wagner, a leading author and spokesman for the church growth movement. Wagner says, "I don't think there is anything intrinsically wrong with the church-growth principles we've developed, or the evangelistic techniques we are using. Yet somehow they don't seem to work . . . maybe something else is needed."[22] Based on statistics and research, Wagner is right—something else is needed.

CHURCH GROWTH IS NOT PEOPLE GROWTH

The most alarming analysis against the church growth movement is that it is possible to grow a church and not grow people. David Dunlap states,

> *A church may be increasing in numbers and to many may seem to be successful, but at the same time be utterly destitute of spiritual life and health. Above all else, genuine growth and renewal must be concerned with the spiritual condition of the church, and not just its programs, music and approach.*[23]

Bill Hybels, pastor of Willow Creek Community Church, one of the largest churches in North America, discovered this a few years ago. After an extensive field research project, he and the leadership team at Willow Creek came to the glaring realization that although they had grown a large church, they were not helping Christians grow. Hybels summarizes the findings: "Some of the stuff that we have put millions of dollars into thinking it would really help our people grow and develop spiritually, when the data actually came back, it wasn't helping people that much."[24]

Bill Hybels refers to the discovery as "the wake-up call" of his adult life and says the leadership of Willow should have placed greater focus on helping people grow.[25] He claims the church leadership made a mistake in that when people became Christians, they did not do a good enough job in helping them grow in their faith. Instead, the church leadership placed their efforts and focus on growing the church numerically, that is, attracting the crowd.

KEEPING THE HORSE BEFORE THE CART

If you think church leaders like Greg Laurie and Bill Hybels are opposed to church growth, you are grossly mistaken. The point they are making is one of focus. When our focus is on church growth, we are not best aligned with our calling. We are called to grow people (Ephesians 4:11–12). We are not called to church growth; we are called to people growth.

When the majority of our time, resources, and efforts is centered on growing churches instead of growing people, something is amiss. The primary focus of church leaders must be on the spiritual condition of the church—growing people, not growing the church.

When we focus on what we are called to do (grow people), God takes care of what we are not called to do (grow churches). When we do our part in helping people grow, the Lord will add to the church daily. We may not have a megachurch, but we can have a growing church.

Laurie states, "Church growth is ultimately God's business, not ours to control."[26] This is clearly seen in the first church. Jesus had already established that He would build His church. Thus, "the first church didn't have a problem with growth because God took care of the growth as they took care of honoring His principles."[27]

Laurie continues, "If there was ever a church growth plan that did work, it was the one the early Christians used. Talk about numbers. Talk about effectiveness. This church exploded. Why? Because they knew why they were here on earth and what they were supposed to do."[28]

The greatest challenge facing church leaders is not increasing the size of the church; the greatest challenge resides in growing the church (people). The greatest growth needed is not church growth, rather the growth of people. And much of the growth of people is the responsibility of church leaders.

WHY DO YOU WANT TO GROW?

DAN ROCKWELL, A LEADERSHIP COACH AND CONSULTANT, tells of a conversation with a friend. His friend knew that Dan regularly interviewed top leadership experts from around the world, so his friend asked, "Had any great interviews lately?"[1] Dan spoke of a recent conversation he had with Claudio Fernández-Aráoz, author of *It's Not the How or the What but the Who*. But much to his surprise, Dan said his friend did not inquire about it. "I was ready to share what I learned from one of the world's top talent experts. But he didn't ask and I didn't say."[2]

In speaking of what occurred, or didn't occur, Dan states, "Any fool can ask the first question"; it is the wise leaders that move beyond the first question and ask the second.[3]

One of the reasons many fail to move beyond the first question is because of self-importance. Dan Rockwell claims, "Big headitis destroys leaders."[4] In contrast, humility and the desire to learn and grow causes leaders to ask the second question. And it is the second question and third question and fourth question and so on that propels leaders beyond mediocrity. Unfortunately, many fail to ask enough questions. Thus, many fail to discover the root cause of problems. Those who desire growth, however, are not content with asking a single question. They will keep asking questions until they discover why something is the way it is.

ASK "WHY?" AGAIN AND AGAIN

How can we ask questions in such a way that we discover things we may not have discovered otherwise? The "5 Whys" technique is one way.

The "5 Whys" technique was invented in the 1930s by Sakichi Toyoda, inventor and founder of Toyota Industries.[5] It was made popular in the 1970s by the Toyota Production System. The strategy involves looking at a problem and asking the why question five times.

It is a simple idea. But by asking the why question repeatedly, a person or group can move beyond the symptoms of a problem and discover the root cause. When the answer to the why question at last cannot be stated, the cause of the problem has likely been identified.[6]

The basis of the "Five Whys" technique can be seen in the fable of the nail and a shoe.

> *For want of a nail a shoe was lost,*
> *for want of a shoe a horse was lost,*
> *for want of a horse a rider was lost,*
> *for want of a rider an army was lost,*
> *for want of an army a battle was lost,*
> *for want of a battle the war was lost,*
> *for want of the war the kingdom was lost,*
> *and all for the want of a little horseshoe nail.*

WHY DO YOU WANT TO GROW?

Asking, "Why was the kingdom lost?" and not stopping with the first or second answer but continuing to dig deep, one would discover it was because of a missing nail in a horseshoe.

The question "Why?" must be asked repeatedly because symptoms often mask the real problem. If all people ever do is address the symptoms of a problem, they will never address the root of the problem. And if the root of a problem is never addressed, the symptoms of the problem will continue to arise. It is only by identifying the root cause of a problem that the symptoms of a problem will cease.

So what does this look like when addressing our stated problem—which is, most churches are declining? Consider the following:

- Why are churches declining? *Answer: People no longer find value in attending church regularly.*
- Why don't people find value in attending church regularly? *Answer: People don't feel challenged, little or no connection to purpose.*
- Why don't people feel challenged? *Answer: They don't understand their place in ministry.*
- Why don't people understand their place in ministry? *Answer: They are not growing.*
- Why are people not growing? *Answer: Because church leaders are trying to grow churches rather than people.*

Although you may arrive at a different conclusion, most church leaders, based on research previously stated, believe the root of the decline of churches is closely associated with the fact that people are not growing. So the next question that should be asked is, "Why aren't people growing?"

If people aren't growing, what's the problem? Who's responsible? According to Paul's writing in Ephesians 4:11–12, the equipping of people is the responsibility of church leaders—namely, the apostles, prophets, evangelists, pastors, and teachers. So why aren't people growing? I suggest it is largely because church leaders have overly invested themselves in matters that are not centered on growing people, and instead are investing time, resources, and energies in trying to grow churches.

But let's not stop there. Let's ask another question. You want church growth—now let's ask why.

Why do you want church growth? The answer is usually closely associated with saving the lost. But what is often overlooked is the underlying motive(s) in wanting the church to grow. For example, consider the following questions and any underlying motives related to church growth:

1. When I compare our growth to the growth of other churches I . . .
    a. am embarrassed.
    b. feel envious.
    c. rejoice, because we are doing better than most.
    d. I don't ever compare my church or ministry to others.
2. If our church experiences growth I will be able to . . .
    a. go fulltime.
    b. hire someone else to help alleviate the load.
    c. build a bigger building.
    d. give more away than what I am already giving.
3. If only I could _____ then we could experience growth.
    a. get people to make and keep commitments
    b. get people to submit to my leadership
    c. get people to be faithful
    d. help people grow and empower them

4. I often resort to using incentives or coercion to get people to . . .
    a. teach a Sunday school class.
    b. get involved in evangelism.
    c. give in tithe and offering.
    d. attend Wednesday night Bible study.
5. True or false: I almost always gauge my effectiveness in speaking by the verbal response of the people.

If you carefully consider these questions, you might discover your desire for church growth is closely associated with a desire to be known; to obtain success in the way we often measure it; and so on. Although few of us are willing to admit it, many of our desires for church growth are closely associated with our ego. We are tempted to be self-sufficient, to be independent, to be spectacular, and to be powerful.

WHO AM I TRYING TO IMPRESS

Wanting to accomplish something great for God seems like a pure and upright motive. But is it? We have been told we need to be like David—step out onto our battlefields and defeat giants! I have even preached messages of the sort. But David didn't go looking for a giant to kill. He was on a mission from his father. Neither did David go looking for a bear and a lion. He was just simply taking care of his father's sheep. I know it makes for good sermons, but we are not called to greatness.

Jesus spoke against desiring greatness. He said,

> *You know that the rulers of the Gentiles lord it over them, and those who are great exercise authority over them. Yet it shall not be so among you; but whoever desires to become great among you, let him be your servant. And whoever desires to be first among*

> you, let him be your slave—just as the Son of Man did not come to be served, but to serve, and to give His life a ransom for many.[7]

Jesus taught that God measures greatness by how many people we serve, not by how many people serve us. We are not called to greatness; we are called to serve and serve faithfully.

Likewise, Paul taught that we are to serve the interests of others above our own. He said, "Let nothing be done through selfish ambition or conceit, but in lowliness of mind let each esteem others better than himself. Let each of you look out not only for his own interests, but also for the interests of others."[8]

Peter echoed the instructions of Jesus in stating that church leaders should "shepherd the flock of God which is among you, serving as overseers, not by compulsion but willingly, not for dishonest gain but eagerly; nor as being lords over those entrusted to you, but being examples to the flock."[9]

Throughout Scripture church leaders are not called to be great, or to accomplish great things, or to do a great work for God; instead, over and over again they are called to serve and to serve faithfully.

Let's be honest. How many of you desire to be a great preacher, to pastor a large and growing church, and so on? Now ask why. Can you honestly state it has nothing to do with you becoming well-known, feeling as though you have accomplished something worthwhile, being asked to preach at conferences, or having your calendar fully booked? I hope you can say it has nothing to do with such things, because many cannot.

THE STRUGGLE WITH EGO IS REAL

A few years after I had resigned the pastorate of a small church, God confronted me one Sunday with my need for healing—specifically, He used someone to say to me, "God wants to heal you." At first I was unsure about that statement, but then the reason dawned on me. God wanted to heal me from feeling like a failure. I had never acknowledged it until that moment, but in my heart that was exactly what I felt. I felt like a failure. We had failed to achieve greatness. The congregation was not large; in fact, it was almost nonexistent. Others did not acknowledge us as having done a great work. In fact, very few said anything.

Exactly one week later, I found myself in an impromptu meeting after a Sunday evening service. It took place in the senior pastor's office along with several other ministers and wives. A guest minister, who had just finished speaking in the church service, said, "I feel this church is at a pivotal moment in time. God wants to bring healing to this church and propel you into a place you have never been before. But it starts with you. In this room there are people who need God to heal them but for that to happen you have to be vulnerable. You have to be willing to stretch forth the hand that needs a touch from God." Then he said, "Who is willing?"

Needless to say, I was somewhat in a state of shock. Not only had someone just the week before said to me, "God wants to heal you," later that same evening that person had told me they felt as though God had brought the church to a pivotal moment in time in which He wanted to administer healing. Within seven days, two ministers had unknowingly stated the same thing.

Yet in spite of this knowledge, I did not go first. My wife did. She raised her hand and said, "I need healing." God was doing an incredible work in her life and that moment proved to be another stepping stone. The guest minister was used of the Lord to minister to her. He then said, "Who is next? Who is willing to allow God to bring healing to you?"

Knowing the events of the previous week, along with seeing my wife's boldness, I raised my hand. I said, "I feel like I was a failure when pastoring a small home missions church." Now, not only had I acknowledged it to myself, my peers knew how I felt. What transpired next shocked me. Instead of the guest minister telling me that I was not a failure, instead of reassuring me that I had done a good job, instead of trying to build up my ego, he looked at me and said, "That is pride, and if you do not get it out of your heart it will send you to hell!"

Although I did not want to admit it, he was right. Pride caused me to feel as if I was a failure. Pride was why I wished the church had grown. Yes, there are other reasons as well, such as I didn't want to see people lost and I wanted to accomplish something great for God. But pride also had something to do with it. I wanted to do well. I wanted to achieve success. I wanted others to think well of me. He was right; it was pride.

Tim Keller, in his book *The Freedom of Self-Forgetfulness* (I highly recommend that every church leader read his book), states,

> *The ego often hurts. That is because it has something incredibly wrong with it. Something unbelievably wrong with it. It is always drawing attention to itself—it does so every single day. It is always making us think about how we look and how we are treated. People sometimes say their feelings are hurt. But our feelings can't be hurt! It is the ego that hurts—my sense of self, my identity. Our feelings are fine! It is my ego that hurts.*[10]

Keller continues by making the point that the way "the normal human ego tries to fill its emptiness and deal with its discomfort is by comparing itself to other people. All the time."[11]

He is right. We aren't supposed to compare ourselves to others, but we do it all the time. This is how we build our ego.

WHY DO YOU WANT TO GROW?

But this is not what Paul taught. Paul's approach to dealing with his ego was unlike our approach. Notice what Paul said in I Corinthians 3:21–4:7.

> *Therefore let no one boast in men. For all things are yours: whether Paul or Apollos or Cephas, or the world or life or death, or things present or things to come—all are yours. And you are Christ's, and Christ is God's.*
>
> *Let a man so consider us, as servants of Christ and stewards of the mysteries of God. Moreover it is required in stewards that one be found faithful. But with me it is a very small thing that I should be judged by you or by a human court. In fact, I do not even judge myself. For I know of nothing against myself, yet I am not justified by this; but He who judges me is the Lord. Therefore judge nothing before the time, until the Lord comes, who will both bring to light the hidden things of darkness and reveal the counsels of the hearts. Then each one's praise will come from God.*
>
> *Now these things, brethren, I have figuratively transferred to myself and Apollos for your sakes, that you may learn in us not to think beyond what is written, that none of you may be puffed up on behalf of one against the other. For who makes you differ from another? And what do you have that you did not receive? Now if you did indeed receive it, why do you boast as if you had not received it?*

Basing his comments on Paul's writings in I Corinthians 3:21–4:7, Keller notes the following:

> *Paul is saying something astounding. "I don't care what you think and I don't care what I think." He is bringing us into*

> *new territory that we know nothing about. His ego is not puffed up, it is filled up. He is talking about humility—although I hate using the word "humility" because this is nothing like our idea of humility. Paul is saying that he has reached a place where his ego draws no more attention to itself than any other part of his body. He has reached the place where he is not thinking about himself anymore.*[12]

I am not there yet. I have yet to reach the place where I do not think about myself anymore. My ego still gets hurt. But I want to reach the place that Paul did. I want my motives to be right.

CRITICISM AND EGO

As church leaders, we often face criticism. Not everyone is going to like the decisions we make. Not everyone is going to appreciate the stance we take. Not everyone is going to like what we preach as well as how we preach. We are going to encounter many possibilities to be hurt and offended by people. And the amount of ego that we allow to live within us will largely determine how we handle such tests.

Keller states that the "self-forgetful person would never be hurt particularly badly by criticism."[13]

> *It would not devastate them, it would not keep them up late, it would not bother them. Why? Because a person who is devastated by criticism is putting too much value on what other people think, on other people's opinions. The world tells the person who is thin-skinned and devastated by criticism to deal with it by saying, "Who cares what they think? I know what I think. Who cares what the rabble thinks? It doesn't bother me." People are either devastated by criticism—or they are not devastated by criticism because they do not listen to it. They will*

not listen to it or learn from it because they do not care about it. They know who they are and what they think. In other words, our only solution to low self-esteem is pride. But that is no solution. Both low self-esteem and pride are horrible nuisances to our own future and to everyone around us.[14]

In contrast, a person who has gotten beyond his ego is the complete opposite. When someone no longer is driven by ego, criticism no longer devastates him. But neither does it result in a hardness that enables him to deal with criticism. Instead, a person who has dealt properly with his ego will listen to criticism, viewing it as an opportunity to change. And some, like myself, allow the lack of church growth to cause us to feel like a failure. That too is rooted closely with issues with our ego.

OVERCOME EGO WITH HUMILITY

What if your entire ministry had more in common with Jeremiah's ministry than Peter's or Paul's? Jeremiah lived in the final days of the crumbling nation of Judah. He was the last prophet sent to preach to the southern kingdom, Judah. God had sent many prophets to warn Israel of their idolatrous ways, but they would not listen. Jeremiah tried to get the people to embrace a fear of God, to trust Him, to place their faith and hope in Him. But the people took God for granted and did not believe Jeremiah.

It is easy to read Jeremiah's story. It would be much more difficult to live it. Jeremiah preached for forty years and never experienced success. No one repented. No one changed. Things continued to digress the entire time he ministered. Jeremiah tried to turn a people toward God but his efforts were in vain. In the end, he had nothing to show for his efforts. "He was called to a ministry of failure."[15]

Who among us would willingly embrace such a ministry? We want success. We want to be recognized by our peers as having accomplished something. We want our investment in ministry to be worthwhile. We want it to make a difference. In other words, we want to be great.

The apostle Paul warned us of these desires. Paul said in Romans 12:3, "For I say, through the grace given to me, to everyone who is among you, not to think of himself more highly than he ought to think, but to think soberly, as God has dealt to each one a measure of faith."[16]

Interestingly, those who have no desire to be great are often the very people who end up achieving great things. Jim Collins, in his book *Good to Great: Why Some Companies Make the Leap . . . and Others Don't*, maintains great leaders demonstrate great humility.[17] In Collins's research of leaders who led good organizations to become great organizations, he discovered the "leaders never wanted to become larger-than-life heroes"; rather, they "were seemingly ordinary people quietly producing extraordinary results."[18]

Jesus taught the least would be the greatest.[19] Those who were not seeking after greatness would become great. This is totally opposite of the way our world operates. And sadly, it is often opposite of how much of the church world operates. Which causes me to ask, "Could it be this is the reason that while there are many good churches, there are not many great ones?"

It is somewhat ironic that although we maintain our desire to do something great for God stems from the purest of motives, we tend to focus more on doing great things for God rather than focusing on Him doing great things in us.

Is it possible our desire to grow great churches is actually keeping us from growing great churches? Perhaps we should consider letting go of the desire for greatness. Perhaps we should simply desire to be faithful to what He has called us to do.

CONCLUSION

The desire for greatness destroys many church leaders. Some, because of unresolved issues with ego, are unethical. Some abuse the power they have been granted. Some take what is not theirs to take, failing the test of ill-gotten gain. Some, in an attempt to increase the size of their church, seek to build relationships with members of other churches. Some are discouraged at the lack of church growth and leave the place where God planted them. Some walk away from ministry, discouraged and disheartened. And the root cause for much of the above is simply unresolved issues with the ego.

Do you have a drive in life to be better than mediocre, to do something great for God, to be great for God? If so, while that may sound noble, it may be self-serving. It may stem from pride. It may be your ego that is driving you. Do you see how deceptive the heart is?[20]

ARE YOU ALIGNED WITH GOD'S PLAN?

WHAT IS GOD'S PLAN FOR GROWTH EXACTLY? Do we have a role to fulfill in it? Do we have any responsibilities? If so, what are they?

These questions and more need to be considered when addressing the subject of growth. Why? Because the way we view things—our paradigms—might cause us to read into Scripture what Scripture is not stating.

As has already been stated, we are not called to grow churches. In fact, nowhere in Scripture will you read anything of the sort. Our God-called purpose is not to increase the size of our congregations. That may or may not happen. We will not be held responsible for the size of the church. We will be judged according to our faithfulness in fulfilling our responsibility.

What is that responsibility? What exactly are we called to do? What role are we to fulfill in God's plan?

JESUS AND CHURCH GROWTH

Jesus stated in Matthew 16:18, "On this rock I will build My church." Notice who Jesus said would do the building: He will. Notice whose church it is: It is His church, and He is the one who will build it.

Simple? Yes, simple. So why do so many church leaders believe they are responsible for building the church? Why do so many church leaders act as though His church is their church?

Notice His method for building His church. Jesus invested the majority of His time in the development of others, namely, the disciples. His method for church growth was the growth of people. Likewise, we are called to make disciples. We are called to equip people. We are called to help people grow. We are not called to church growth; we are called to people growth.

Is this a valid model for the church today? I believe so. In fact, I am certain it is, especially in light of the fact that our model of church growth has not yielded the results needed. Perhaps we should consider doing things differently than we have been doing them. Perhaps we should return to the old paths, the tried and proven way. His way. After all, it is His church. And He said He would build it.

PAUL AND CHURCH GROWTH

That church growth is not our responsibility is echoed in Paul's writings as well as practice. Paul stated in I Corinthians 3:5–6, "Who then is Paul, and who is Apollos, but ministers through whom you believed, as the Lord gave to each one? I planted, Apollos watered, but God gave the increase." Paul understood his responsibility. He was not responsible for church growth; God was the one who gave the increase. Paul was responsible for planting.

Some claim Paul started fourteen churches during his lifetime; others think the number may have been closer to twenty, and possibly more. Interestingly, Roland Allen, in *Missionary Methods: St. Paul's or*

ARE YOU ALIGNED WITH GOD'S PLAN?

Ours?, maintains Paul's overarching goal was not planting churches that would become big; but rather planting churches that would plant other churches.[1] Paul was not as concerned about church growth as he was with the growth of people who would be instrumental in the expansion of the church elsewhere. And this is exactly what occurred.

That the apostle Paul was not focused on church growth, rather the growth of people, is most fascinating. And this is the guy whom many of us view as a church growth specialist. Rather than focus on church growth, Paul's writings are filled with instruction that focuses on the growth of people. He does not write about church growth. Paul understood the principle that if you help people grow, church growth will take care of itself. Church growth is about people growth. In Paul's method for church growth, growing people generates growing churches.

Paul's focus on the growth of people is seen in his writings in I Thessalonians 3:12–4:12. Paul began by stating that he prayed for the believers of the church of Thessalonica, that their love would increase and overflow for everyone, that they would be blameless and holy. He then instructed the believers to live life in such a way that it pleased God, to be holy, to avoid sexual immortality, to control their own bodies in a way that was holy and honorable, to avoid wronging their spiritual brother or taking advantage of him, to love their spiritual brother more than ever, to lead a quiet life, to mind their own business, and to work with their hands so that they might win the respect of outsiders. Paul was focusing on the growth of believers, not on church growth.

In I Thessalonians 5:12–15, Paul spoke of respecting leaders. He warned of being idle. He instructed believers to encourage the timid, to help the weak, to be patient with everyone, to pay back no one's wrong with another wrong, and to be kind to one another as well as everyone else.

Paul gave similar instructions in letters written to the believers of other churches. Paul's efforts were clearly centered on growing people, not on growing churches. Based on such, if Paul were alive today I doubt he would invest much of his time crafting a clever marketing scheme, new logo, website, sound system, church building, choir, Sunday school program, special event, and so on. Paul's primary focus was on growing people. If living today, I suspect his primary focus would be the same.

Please do not misunderstand me. I am not saying these things are wrong, that we should not care about our websites or our business cards or our multimedia announcements. I am simply stating that such things should not be our primary focus. Either we can spend an enormous amount of time, energy, resources, and focus on things that are geared to growing churches, or we can invest ourselves in equipping people. Clearly, Paul's focus was on the growth of people— and it worked. I submit that what worked then will work now. Paul did what you and I should be doing, that is, if we want to see growth. He prayed for the believers. He implored them to be holy and loving and then instructed them how to do so. His efforts were focused on growing people and helping people become equipped for ministry.

WE ARE CALLED TO EQUIP OTHERS

As previously stated, nowhere in the Bible will you find that we are called to grow churches. Nowhere. And yet that is precisely what many of us are trying to do. However, that is not our purpose; that is not our calling.

The apostle Paul defined our purpose in Ephesians 4:11–12: "And He Himself gave some to be apostles, some prophets, some evangelists, and some pastors and teachers, for the equipping of the saints for the work of ministry, for the edifying of the body of Christ."

ARE YOU ALIGNED WITH GOD'S PLAN?

Paul, in describing the purpose of the fivefold ministry as equipping or preparing people, used the Greek word *katartismon*.[2] This same word, *katartismon*, is used elsewhere in Scripture, and it always conveys the "idea of making things or people what they ought to be."[3] Unfortunately, some leaders are attempting to equip people (to make people what they ought to be) for the wrong purpose.

Some church leaders think equipping others involves getting people do the things to grow the church. This is not the idea behind equipping others. The goal is not to get people to do things or to act in ways we think are necessary to grow the church, or to have great church services that grow the church or get people saved. The goal of church leaders should be to help people grow, to help people become what they ought to be, not to do the things we think they ought to do. If we will help people become what they ought to be, they will do what they ought to do. And, consequently, God will add to the church.

The Greek word, *katartismon*, translated as "equip" in Ephesians 4:12, is used in its verb form, *katartizo*, in Matthew 4:21.[4] Jesus was walking along the Sea of Galilee and saw Peter, Andrew, James, and John sitting in a boat mending (*katartizo*) their nets. Peter, Andrew, James, and John were "equipping their nets by mending them. They were fixing their nets, making them strong, preparing them for service, getting them ready for action."[5]

This is what we are called to do. We are not called to grow churches, to increase the size of our congregations. We are called to get people ready for action, to prepare them for service, to equip people for the work of ministry. (I address this more fully in my book *Realign: God-Called Leaders Connecting with Their Purpose*.)

Paul claimed every member of the body has been given a gift. And it is the responsibility of church leaders to help equip people to function within their gift. Church leaders are responsible for equipping others, for helping people change, for helping people grow, for helping people discover and develop the gifts God has given them.

EVERYONE IS TO BE INVOLVED IN MINISTRY

Oftentimes the reason church leaders struggle with getting others to commit, to help carry the load, is that church leaders won't relinquish control of things. God never intended for people to sit on church pews while watching church leaders perform.

Unfortunately, this is often the common practice in many churches—church leaders perform while everyone else watches. Church leaders do the work of ministry, and everyone else reaps the benefits. This is not the way ministry is supposed to work. The responsibility of church leadership is to equip others as workers. Everyone is to be involved in ministry.

Church leaders who believe they are in charge of everything and that everyone else exists to help them perform their ministry adhere to an outdated church model that is based on the Old Testament priest carrying the load of ministry. But according to I Peter 2:9, we are all priests. Everyone gets to participate in the work of ministry. Everyone is given a gift and each one is to utilize the gift God has given him or her. Everyone is to be involved in ministry.

> *The New Testament concept of the pastor is not of a person who jealously guards all ministries in his own hands, and successfully squashes all lay initiatives, but of one who helps and encourages all God's people to discover, develop and exercise their gifts. His teaching and training are directed to this end, to enable the people of God to be a servant people, ministering actively but humbly according to their gifts. Thus, instead of monopolizing all ministries for himself, he actually multiplies ministries.[6]*

The goal of a church leader must not be in trying to do the bulk of ministry. That is an outdated mode and certainly not the original model. The goal of a church leader should be to align with his God-called purpose. The focus should be on developing people and letting them use their gifts to fulfill their ministry. This is how church expansion occurs—not from focusing on church growth.

WHAT DO MY ACTIONS REVEAL?

Perhaps you're thinking, *I get it. I understand the importance of growing people, and I am committed to that end.* But are your actions aligned with your commitment? Sometimes what we say and what we do are contrary to one another. For example, we say we want others to get involved in ministry but then we do most of the ministry. We say we want others to take ownership of things and then we act as though we are afraid to let others take the lead.

Church leaders set expectations by their actions, not their words. When church leaders attempt to do all the work of ministry, others will watch. When church leaders seek to control and micromanage the work of ministry, others will become frustrated and will not engage fully. Sadly, many church leaders bemoan the lack of involvement and commitment of people but fail to equip and empower people to do the work of ministry.

Consider the following—ask yourself:

- Do I place more emphasis on church programs than on making disciples of Jesus? In fact, when was the last time I deleted a church program and didn't replace it with another program?
- Am I more concerned about attracting people with a fancy sermon than about teaching people to be followers

of Christ, to be students of the Bible, to understand the importance of theology?
- Am I more concerned with plans to build a bigger building, buy more land, market the church, and so on, than I am with releasing others to minister within the community?
- Am I prone to drive people in an attempt to grow the church, or do I believe God will add to the church daily such as should be saved?
- Am I striving to build my ministry, or am I mostly concerned with building the ministry of others?
- Am I likely to ask too much of people, burning them out? Or do I understand that, for many people, one of the greatest ministry opportunities they have is at their place of employment?
- Does everything have to cross my desk for approval? Am I building a culture in which the success of the church is entirely dependent upon me, or do I seek to empower others? Do I allow others to make decisions and stand by those decisions even though they may not be the decision I would have made?
- Am I more likely to preach allegorical messages in an attempt to wow people, or do I do my best to stay true to the text even though it may not elicit a great response from the people?
- Do I add to the Word of God things the Word of God is not saying in order to support my opinion? Or am I careful in dictating to others my opinions, understanding that adding to the Word of God is harmful and detrimental to their growth?
- Am I driven to see the church grow so I can become better known, to acquire a position, and perhaps one day leave

to pastor a larger church? Or am I mostly concerned with seeing people grow and excel in all God has called them to be?

Such questions, if carefully considered, may reveal actions not aligned with our God-called purpose.

Many church leaders place heavy emphasis on programs. It's not bad to have programs. Healthy congregations usually have multiple programs. But multiple programs does not mean a church is healthy. A problem arises when programs become the ultimate aim rather than a means to the end.

Many church leaders focus on events. Those who do often define success by how many people attend an event. But the reality is this: "The more of a priority you place on events (at the neglect of relationships and discipleship), the more you suffocate your congregation."[7] The problem is not events. The problem is when events become the primary focus rather than a part in the process.

Many church leaders know how to create impactful church services. There is nothing wrong with impactful church services. But, sadly, some church leaders are doing little to help people know what to do to make a difference in the lives of others outside of church services. The problem is not church services. The problem is when we allow church services to become the chief focus rather than a part in the process.

Many church leaders chase after the latest church growth techniques. There is nothing wrong with learning how to be more effective. We ought to do our best with everything we do, from parking lot attendants to lighting to quality of sound and so on. But many know much about church growth techniques and little about how to equip others.

Many church leaders have learned how to social network, how to build a following. There is nothing wrong with using social media. But while some may have learned how to build a personal following, it is something different to build a Jesus following.

Please do not miss the point—many acknowledge they are called to equip people, called to help people grow, called to develop people, but many of the things they do are not aligned with that calling. Why not? Perhaps it is because they are more concerned with growing churches than they are concerned with growing people. Perhaps it is because they believe it is their responsibility to grow churches.

DO I WANT WHAT GOD WANTS?

The root cause of conflict and division (even in our own lives) is our desires. James 4:1–3 states,

> *Where do wars and fights come from among you? Do they not come from your desires for pleasure that war in your members? You lust and do not have. You murder and covet and cannot obtain. You fight and war. Yet you do not have because you do not ask. You ask and do not receive, because you ask amiss, that you may spend it on your pleasures.*

James declares our desires are the root cause for the wars and fights that occur within. What desires? Desires for money, for power, for prestige, for material possessions, and so on.

As church leaders we speak against such things in the hearts and lives of others; however, we must be mindful the same battle rages within our own hearts. We are either aiming for a life that is wholly committed to the will of God, or we are seeking to gratify our own desires. And the root cause of unceasing and bitter conflict in our lives is aiming for the latter.

ARE YOU ALIGNED WITH GOD'S PLAN?

Wanting what God wants means aiming at the target He has given us, regardless of whether or not it generates the success we desire. It means focusing on what He has called us to do, equipping others rather than pushing for church growth. This means we may not acquire power or prestige or possessions. This means our portfolio may not increase. We may not get that bigger house or drive that nicer car. But the only way to eliminate the conflict and division within our own heart is to aim for the right target. Aiming for a target different than what God has given us brings conflict and division into our lives.

When conflict and division rages in our own hearts, it impacts everything we do. If wars and fights within do not cease to exist, they will manifest themselves in our relationships with others. Inward disturbance, if not properly addressed, will in time result in disturbance in our relationships with others.

This is easily seen in the church, even amongst church leaders. "The rivalry and competition within the church is undeniable."[8] It is often seen in local churches among leaders who are enamored with the senior pastoral position. It happens among local pastors, each one trying to outdo the other. It is seen within parachurch organizations as members politic for coveted positions of leadership. Rivalry and competition in the church are birthed out of inward desires.

William Barclay states,

> *When all men are striving to possess the same things, life inevitably becomes a competitive arena. They trample each other down in the rush to grasp them. They will do anything to eliminate a rival. Obedience to the will of God draws men together, for it is that will that they should love and serve one another; obedience to the craving for pleasure drives men apart, for it drives them to internecine rivalry for the same things.*[9]

Aiming at the wrong target causes many problems. When we aim for the wrong target we "become blind to who we are in Christ, and blind to what the church is supposed to be."[10] And, according to James, when we take aim at the wrong target our prayers go unanswered.

Barclay, in reference to James 4:1-3, says,

> *The craving for pleasure in the end shuts the door of prayer. If a man's prayers are simply for the things which will gratify his desires, they are essentially selfish and, therefore, it is not possible for God to answer them. The true end of prayer is to say to God, "Thy will be done." The prayer of the man who is pleasure dominated is: "My desires be satisfied." It is one of the grim facts of life that a selfish man can hardly ever pray aright; no one can ever pray aright until he removes self from the center of his life and puts God there. In this life we have to choose whether to make our main object our own desires or the will of God. And, if we choose our own desires, we have thereby separated ourselves from our fellowmen and from God.*[11]

Is it possible that the reason some churches are not experiencing growth—increasing in size—is because some church leaders are trying to grow churches rather than people? Is it possible that some church leaders are greatly frustrated because they are aiming for the wrong target? It certainly seems so.

When we elevate our own desires over the desires of God, we impede what God wants to do in our lives. We also impede the work God wants to do through us. When we elevate our own desires over the desires of God, we will ask and not receive. When we elevate our own desires over the desires of God, we will experience frustration.

5

MEASURING GROWTH

AS A SMALL CHILD, I remember the church scoreboard. It was located on the back wall of the sanctuary where my grandfather, Elmer Jenkins, was the pastor. It served as a constant reminder of the current state of the church, whether or not things were going well or not so well. With just a simple glance one could see the attendance of the day, attendance of last Sunday, as well as today's offering and the offering from a week ago. It also displayed the record attendance. The scoreboard let us know if we were winning or losing.

Grandpa also served for twenty-seven years as the Indiana District UPCI Sunday school director. I have many fond memories as a child attending children's camps and seeing my grandpa ring an old farm bell to announce it was time to eat. Serving in this capacity was actually an outflow of what Grandpa placed focus on at the church where he served as pastor. As a child I remember candy rains from the church's rooftop; someone riding a horse down the center aisle of the sanctuary; backwards Sunday, in which everyone wore their hair on the opposite side and clothes were worn backwards (one man drove his car backwards to church, howbeit, only a couple of blocks); and on old fashioned Sunday, when everyone dressed as if they were attending church in the 1800s. And the purpose of such things was to increase the attendance, to win.

Unfortunately, many are still using the same scoreboard—perhaps not one that is hung on the wall somewhere (although, occasionally I come across them), but maybe one of a different type, usually something on a computer. And the focus is nearly always on the number of attendees and dollars.

GET RID OF THE OLD SCOREBOARD

David Ferguson, lead pastor of Community, a multi-site church in Chicago, says he is on a mission to explode the old scoreboard.[1] He lists two problems with the old scoreboard: (1) "It is entirely possible for a church's attendance to be growing, while the kingdom of God is shrinking," and (2) "It is entirely possible for a church's attendance to be growing, but the impact of the church is shrinking."[2]

Ferguson states,

> *Right now, there are more people attending church on any given weekend in the United States than ever before! We could conclude that U.S. church attendance is growing and therefore we must be winning, right? Wrong! While there are more people attending church than ever before, a smaller percentage of the total population in every state in the country is attending church than ever before.*[3]

Ferguson maintains that even if attendance is increasing, "that stat completely ignores other vital statistics."[4] So what if attendance is up if lives are not being changed? So what if attendance is up but people are not growing in their relationship with God? So what if attendance

MEASURING GROWTH

is up if the community in which the church people live is not being impacted? If attendance is increasing but people are not discovering God's purpose in their life and actively engaging in their ministry, what good is increased attendance?

This is not to say there is something ineluctably wrong with numbers. Acts 1:15 records the number of people filled with the Holy Spirit in the upper room was about 120; in Acts 2:41 about 3,000 were added to the church. However, the early church did not take the number of people filled with the Holy Spirit or added to the church out of context.

Neither should numbers be taken out of context today. Numbers should not be used to promote individual ministries, to propagandize pastors of growing churches, or to be used in ways in which we brag on the churches we lead. It's not about the number; it's about the people.

Numbers can offer great value, however, if used in a constructive way. For example, numbers should be looked at closely when associated with the "why" question. Why did the church decline in attendance over the past five years? Why did one hundred people experience the new birth this past year but only three remain in the church? Numbers should move us toward why questions. In this way, numbers are of immense value.

But, sadly, in many churches "numbers only represent an increase in the number of people who have joined the spectators."[5] The church needs more than mere spectators if it is to be what God meant for it to be. A church that makes a difference in the world must consist of people who are willing to get on the playing field. Surely God has something more in mind for those who were added to the church than to be mere spectators. Adding spectators may increase the size of the congregation, but it will not advance the kingdom of God.

And yet the number of attendees and dollars remains the most common gauge by which we measure effectiveness of ministry. What if there was a better way? What if there was a more viable way of measuring things? The fivefold ministry is called to equip others for their work of ministry. Is it possible to identify a form(s) of measurement more aligned with that calling? I believe so.

A NEW SCOREBOARD

The first crucial step in establishing a new scoreboard is identifying the target. As Christians we are called to make disciples; and as members of the fivefold ministry we are called to equip others for their work of ministry. The first step, therefore, is to identify the target—what is a disciple? What is an equipped saint? What does discipleship consist of? What does an equipped saint do?

If you haven't identified what a mature disciple is, how will you know when someone has become one? If you have not established a pathway or strategy for growing others, how will others know what the next step is? If you have not identified what an equipped saint is, how do you expect to equip others?

These are just a few questions that should be considered. There are more. We need a scoreboard that involves more than attendance and giving. Why? Because our goal is neither to increase attendance nor increase giving. Our goal is to make disciples who make disciples; our goal is to equip others for their work of ministry. Our scoreboard ought to reflect our purpose.

Several years ago a couple that had recently become Christians met with me concerning some difficulties in their marriage. It was the third marriage for both. Being a blended family as well as having baggage from the past, they had great challenges to say the least. I met with this couple quite extensively for a period of time. Thankfully, they grew in their relationship with God as well as with each other, became active members in the church, and in time found a place in which to serve in ministry. A few years later the wife said to me,

MEASURING GROWTH

> *I love to hear good preaching. But when we were new believers and struggling in establishing our marriage and getting beyond our baggage, we needed more than good preaching. If that were all we would have had, we would have never made it. We needed someone to get down in the trenches and fight with us.*

The old scoreboard misses this point. It places emphasis on increasing attendance. It places emphasis on increasing the amount of dollars given in the offering. The old scoreboard does little to place the focus on helping couples like the one I just described. It does little to help people grow, little to help people discover their place in ministry. The old scoreboard places emphasis on the wrong things. It does not reflect our goal—making disciples, equipping others for their work of ministry. The new scoreboard must place emphasis on discipling and equipping.

Another crucial step in establishing a new scoreboard is identifying the process whereby people become disciples and are equipped for their work of ministry. Some seem to think people become disciples and are equipped solely, or mostly, through the programs a church offers. But one of the chief problems with programs is that they often result in people serving programs rather than the programs serving the people. Unfortunately, this happens too frequently as church leaders urge people to attend and commit to programs. Sadly, the message conveyed is that the programs matter more than the people.

Discipling and equipping others involves doing the messy work of getting to know people where they are. This best happens through relationships; it must involve people connecting with others. Real discipleship "disrupts the routine and calls people to reassess their priorities. Real discipleship changes the conversation and infiltrates every aspect of life."[6] It occurs when a person disciples another person. It should be of no surprise that Jesus invested most of His ministry into discipling twelve men. Changing the lives of others involves much more than standing behind a pulpit and telling people what to do.

An example of a model for developing people, a five-step process, is found in Dave and Jon Ferguson's book, *Exponential*:[7]

> Step one: I do. You watch. We talk.
> Step two: I do. You help. We talk.
> Step three: You do. I help. We talk.
> Step four: You do. I watch. We talk.
> Step five: You do. Someone else watches.

What I particularly like about Ferguson's model is how he measures success. Ferguson states, "Because of our commitment to people development and leadership development, we keep track of and report every month how many apprenticeships are taking place and what percentage of our leaders have apprentices."[8] Because of a commitment to discipling and equipping, diligence is given to tracking the process—primarily, how many apprenticeships are taking place and what percentage of leaders have apprenticeships.

Thus, the new scoreboard does not cease counting things; instead, it seeks to count the right things for the right reasons. In keeping track of how many apprenticeships are taking place as well as what is the percentage of leaders who have apprentices, Ferguson offers a valid alternative to the traditional forms of measurement. Ferguson states, "I've heard people say you can't measure discipleship. But I'm not sure that's entirely true. It is true that you can't necessarily put a number or percentage on discipleship growth, but you can tell—over time—if it has happened or is happening."[9]

So what should we be looking at? Consider the following: How scalable is your disciple-making process? Do you know who needs to mature but is not maturing? Do you know who has stalled?

Leaders tend to focus on what they measure. While attendance and giving matters, there are other things that matter more. But, unfortunately, we are not measuring them. Attendance and dollars given should not be the chief focus of our discipling and equipping effort. "We say we value people more than money, but we count money down to the penny and estimate people."[10] If you aren't tracking ministry effectiveness in the community, life change within groups, and leadership development, you are missing the point and are in need of a new scoreboard.

Those who continue to adhere to the old scoreboard, one that focuses primarily on number of attendees and dollars in the plate, will do what is necessary to keep the numbers up and moving in the right direction. They will be tempted to embellish the actual number counted because they feel as though there were more people in the crowd. "As a result, the numbers they rely on to determine the vitality of the church become little more than educated guesses."[11]

Why do some resist ascertaining measurements in the areas that really matter? Perhaps it is because measuring intangibles such as leadership development and community involvement paints a painfully accurate picture of the status of the church. This may be why many church leaders would rather not measure these numbers. However, if equipping God's people for works of service is the talk of your church, shouldn't it also be the criteria by which the health of your church is determined?[12] I think so.

HOW CAN WE KNOW PEOPLE ARE GROWING?

It is easier to count how many people are in attendance or how much was given in the offering than it is to clearly identify if people are involved in discipleship and becoming equipped. However, this does not negate the importance of establishing a new scoreboard.

LEADING GROWTH

A new and improved scoreboard may not be able to identify solid measurements involving numbers like the old scoreboard. However, there are principles we can adhere to that can help us know if we are moving in the right direction regarding building disciples and equipping others for their work of ministry.

Consider the following principles as indications of whether or not discipleship is occurring:[13]

- Those who have been in the church the longest complain the least. – *Do everything without complaining or arguing* (Philippians 2:14).
- The leaders of the church are most likely to give up "their" seats, park further from the building, or do whatever is necessary to help the Body. – *The greatest among you must be a servant* (Matthew 23:11).
- The church celebrates most when those far from faith come to faith. *In the same way, there is more joy in heaven over one lost sinner who repents and returns to God than over ninety-nine others who are righteous and haven't strayed away!* (Luke 15:7).
- Members care that others' needs are met more than their own. *Don't look out only for your own interests, but take an interest in others, too* (Philippians 2:4).
- There is joy even during suffering – *Consider it pure joy, my brothers and sisters, whenever you face trials of many kinds* (James 1:2).
- The teaching is a balance of truth and grace. *Jesus came full of grace and truth* (John 1:17).
- The financial needs of the church are funded, with people willingly sacrificing. No one begs for money. *Each person*

should do as he has decided in his heart–not reluctantly or out of necessity, for God loves a cheerful giver (II Corinthians 9:7).
- There are no petty disputes and grudges among the people of the church. *Therefore encourage one another and build each other up* (I Thessalonians 5:11).
- The church takes care of each other well. *There was not a needy person among them, for as many as were owners of lands or houses sold them and brought the proceeds of what was sold* (Acts 4:34).

There are other principles and indications of whether or not people are growing. Jesus said in John 13:35, "By this all will know that you are My disciples, if you have love for one another." Paul described the characteristics of a person who is filled with the Holy Spirit as fruit: "But the fruit of the Spirit is love, joy, peace, longsuffering, kindness, goodness, faithfulness, gentleness, self-control" (Galatians 5:22–23).

The point is this—a new scoreboard is needed and it will not look like the old one. Instead of focus being given to the number of attenders or the amount in the offering, the primary focus will be on whether or not people are growing.

HOW CAN WE KNOW THAT WE ARE DEVELOPING LEADERS?

Although measuring the number of leaders who are being developed is a better measurement than the number of attendees on Sunday service, we can do even better than that. Paul addressed the qualifications for leadership in the church in I Timothy 3:2–12 and Titus 1:6–9. His focus was on heart issues, not leadership ability. Furthermore, Paul's writings suggest that the heart issues of a potential leader are not abstract; they can be seen in a leader's relationship with his spouse, children, others, finances, and so on.

The makings or elements needed to measure the right thing exist. The challenge is that we have not given attention to them. For example, when it comes to leadership development, we are more likely to celebrate the number of young leaders attending a leadership class than we are to the quality of development occurring in their lives. Why? Because it is much easier to do the former than the latter, and an increase in number makes us feel good.

Instead of focusing on the quantity of young leaders being developed, we should seek to measure the quality of young leaders: are they living what they talk, orbiting around the common purpose, faithfully serving, celebrating the success of others, supporting one another, mentoring others, not lording over others, and remaining humble when given positions and titles? The point is—a new and improved scoreboard will consist of more than attendance; it will closely reflect the target—a mature and developed leader. These are the things we need to be measuring.

HOW DO WE GAUGE CULTURE?

Culture helps people grow. Culture is also a reflection of people who are growing. And culture is an indicator of whether or not people will experience growth. Thus, culture matters.

Church culture should be of vital concern to church leaders, and they should seek to gauge or measure it. Is the current church culture conducive to the developmental process of people? Is it a healthy culture, one in which developing leaders experience organic growth? Is it a positive culture in which people experience hope and healing?

Most church leaders want the church to grow, and most leaders want people to experience growth. Yet many church leaders are puzzled by why growth is not occurring. In the end, however, healthy things grow. Likewise, unhealthy things do not grow.

MEASURING GROWTH

People don't want to be a part of a toxic culture. When the culture of a church allows gossip, slander, backbiting, rudeness, arguing, fighting, and so on, people will not grow. Growth occurs in healthy cultures. It does not occur in toxic cultures.

So, considering the importance of culture, how does one measure or gauge it? Consider the following culture destroyers:

- Teams meet and talk, but nothing gets done.
- Perks are given based on position. Example, special parking spots for church leaders, gifts for special occasions such as birthdays, anniversaries, and holidays.
- Things that should be dealt with go unaddressed. Example, unethical and immoral behavior among leaders.
- Instead of empowering people, people are micromanaged.
- There is a lack of boundaries; people, especially subordinates, are constantly infringed upon.
- A lack of communication persists. Instead of people being included in the conversation in which decisions are made, they are informed of how things will be.
- Rather than first considering problems as a breakdown in a system or process, people are constantly viewed as the problem.

If such things are occurring, it is doubtful the current culture is best suited for growth. Thus, care must be taken to gauge or measure culture. Why? Because culture impacts the growth of people, teams, and, ultimately, the church as a whole.

Unfortunately, most churches are not ready for growth, nor are they doing what is necessary for growth. Most churches are just trying to make the church bigger.

LEADING GROWTH

HOW HEALTHY IS YOUR PRACTICE OF CULTURE AND TEAM BUILDING?

Peter Scazzero, author of *Emotionally Healthy Spirituality* and *The Emotionally Healthy Church*, offers helpful insight into growth. Scazzero maintains that growth is the result of healthy things, that when things are healthy, growth is the natural byproduct. Scazzero believes church leaders should focus on being healthy, on helping others be healthy, and growth will take care of itself. Furthermore, he recognizes the crucial role culture fulfills in the health of individuals, teams, and congregations.

Scazzero offers the following assessment for measuring the culture of a team, a factor that largely impacts the health of a team, and consequently, the effectiveness of a team.[14]

Use the following scale:

5 = Always true of me
4 = Frequently true of me
3 = Occasionally true of me
2 = Rarely true of me
1 = Never true of me

_____ 1. I invest in key people from my team, both in their transformation in Christ and in their skill or professional development.
_____ 2. I directly and promptly address "elephants in the room" (tensions, lateness, hostile body language, sarcasm, unkind remarks, silence, etc.).
_____ 3. I consider healthy rhythms and loving union with Jesus as the indispensable foundation for building a healthy culture and team.

MEASURING GROWTH

_____ 4. I explore and ask questions when people are highly reactive, or triggered, rather than ignore them.
_____ 5. I negotiate differences, and clarify expectations when there is frustration and conflict.
_____ 6. I communicate in ways that are clear, honest, respectful, and timely.
_____ 7. I intentionally set aside time and space in team meetings to instill particular values (e.g. Scripture, expressing appreciations, sharing new insights on leadership).
_____ 8. I dedicate the necessary time to explore the root causes of inappropriate behavior, seeing it as a spiritual formation opportunity.
_____ 9. People experience me as willing to take the time to "tune in" to them.
_____ 10. I ask specific questions about the quality of people's marriage or singleness because it is a key factor to build a healthy culture and team.

If you scored mostly ones and twos, you probably have not given much thought to, or perhaps received much training in building healthy cultures and teams. Becoming aware of how what you do—and don't do—affects the people around you is an important competency for leadership. You might take a first step by listing the desires and values you have for your team. Consider inviting a trusted team member into your process. Read carefully the four characteristics of healthy culture and team building, picking one to focus on and apply in your own setting.

If you scored mostly twos and threes, you are somewhat engaged in healthy culture and team building. The reasons you're not more engaged could be anything from a lack of priority or vision to an aversion to conflict or a lack of mentoring. I encourage you to take a few hours to prayerfully reflect—alone or with others—on your team and culture. Make a list of the characteristics that presently describe your culture and team. Then make a second list noting the values, desires, and dreams God has given you for your team. Identify three to five specific steps you can take over the next three to nine months to bridge the gap between your current culture and team and the culture and team you envision.

If you scored mostly fours and fives, congratulations! You are building a healthy culture and team and are well positioned to multiply yourself so that others can lead and develop a culture of their own teams. Consider putting your perspectives on healthy culture and teams into writing for others or teaching it to your team so that new staff and volunteers can fully "own" being part of your culture.

For more information, check out Scazzero's latest book, *The Emotionally Healthy Leader*, or website, www.emotionallyhealthy.org.

CONCLUSION

There are many other things that will likely be added in the development of a new scoreboard. I have simply offered these things as a possible starting point, some things to consider. Of this I am certain: the old scoreboard is the least effective measurement, and the new scoreboard must be centered on our purpose—discipling and equipping others for their work of ministry.

LEADERSHIP **STYLES**

THUS FAR WE HAVE ADDRESSED the reality that churches are not growing. We have also addressed the fact that people are not growing. And we have suggested the primary reason people are not growing is because church leaders are not focusing on growing people. Instead, church leaders are concerned with growing the church, something entirely different. We now turn our attention to church leadership styles that enhance the growth of people, and subsequently, increase the likelihood of churches growing the way God intended churches to grow.

A LEADER OF GROWTH

You may doubt your ability to help people grow, to help people discover their gifts, hone their gifts, and be released to function in their gifts while doing the work of ministry. You may think growth is dependent upon resources you do not have and talent you do not possess. If this is how you think, you are wrong. Growth does not hinge on your charisma, oratory ability, or church edifice. The early church was not dependent upon such things; neither is today's church dependent on such things.

So what impacts growth? What factors influence the growth of people and ultimately the growth of congregations? Carey Nieuwhof, in "10 Very Possible Reasons Your Church Isn't Growing," suggests church growth is limited when the following conditions exist:[1]

1. Church members are in conflict with one another, constantly bickering and arguing.
2. The church is holding on to the past, and not reaching for the future.
3. Church members are not enjoyable to be around. They are fake, judgmental, hypocritical, angry, unkind, and so on.
4. The church is too focused on self.
5. The church thinks culture is the enemy.
6. Church leaders are afraid to risk what "is" for the sake of what "might be".
7. Church leaders cannot make a decision.
8. Church leaders talk more than they act.
9. Church leaders and members don't think there's anything wrong with the church.
10. Church leaders are more focused on church growth and have forgotten about the mission.

Nieuwhof presents some interesting possibilities for the lack of church growth, reasons that seem to make sense. Notice, however, the underlying issue, something Nieuwhof—along with most church leaders—fails to acknowledge or recognize. Think about it. The lack of church growth is directly related to the lack of growth in the lives of the church members and church leaders.

DO YOU "GET" IT?

By now you might be tired of hearing me say it. You may be thinking, *You've made your point. Move on.* But there is a reason I keep saying the same thing: What is accepted by the mind is not always accepted in the heart. That is, what we may acknowledge to be the case is not always how we live. In the heat of the moment what is in the heart is usually what is first manifested.

Consider the following story my friend, Jeff Jaco, told me. Jeff hired a church consultant to work with him. The church consultant was of a different faith but had consulted with churches and church leaders of various faiths. His specialty was in helping churches with an average attendance of one thousand people grow their membership lists to several thousand. At the time in which the consultant first began working with Jeff, the church where he served as pastor had an average attendance of less than one hundred.

The following is what Jeff said the consultant told him:

> *Jeff, I've worked with several churches in your organization now and I can tell you that it's not your doctrine that keeps your churches from growing. And it's not your conservative lifestyle that is keeping your churches from growing. It's the fact that your pastors are preachers but not leaders and you must have those who are both to grow a church.*

He went on to tell Jeff that the pastors he had worked with acted as if they wrote the Bible, were headstrong, and were largely resistant to change and to learning how to become a better leader.

Jeff Jaco said while working with this consultant there were times when he thought he was getting what the consultant was saying. But what he thought he understood wasn't always being transferred into action. The consultant asked, "What in the world are you doing?"

LEADING GROWTH

When he tried to explain, the consultant said, "But that's not what you are doing. You are saying one thing but you are doing another." The consultant got in his face and shouted, "Stop trying to grow your church and start growing people!"

Jeff said, "I finally got it." The consultant helped Jeff understand that the key to church growth is not found in focusing on church growth. Rather, it is found in growing a core of leaders and empowering those leaders. Church growth is the result of the growth of people. Church growth happens naturally. The consultant helped him understand that if he would invest in leadership development (equipping others) it would become an investment in the church at large. Jeff said, "I had to hear it over and over again before I really got it."

Perhaps you are thinking, *I understand the point—grow people—I've got it!* But it is likely that you are like Jeff; you need to hear it over and over again.

Look at the people you lead. Are they discipling others? Have you empowered them? Are they being stretched, or are they lethargic and bored with church? Are they faithful and highly committed? Do they understand their gifts? Are they using their gifts to function in ministry? Do you have a pathway for growing people? Do the people you lead clearly understand what that pathway is? Do you and the people you lead know what the target is? Can you articulate what a mature disciples is, how he acts, functions, and so on?

Do you know the answers to these questions? Your responsibility is to equip people. It is your responsibility to empower people. What are you doing to fulfill your responsibility? Is your style of leadership enhancing growth or is it limiting it?

LEADERSHIP DEFINED

There is no one-size-fits-all definition for leadership. For example, some believe leadership is simply influence. Others maintain leadership is identifying what needs to be done and getting others to do the work. Still others point out that leadership involves a process for achieving a common goal.

A robust definition for leadership is that leadership involves a process whereby a person

> selects, equips, trains, and influences one or more follower(s) who have diverse gifts, abilities, and skills and focuses the follower(s) to the organization's mission and objectives causing the follower(s) to willingly and enthusiastically expend spiritual, emotional, and physical energy in a concerted coordinated effort to achieve the organizational mission and objectives.[2]

Henry Blackaby and Richard Blackaby, in *Spiritual Leadership*, suggest "spiritual leadership" is the process by which people are led away from their own plans and become centered on fulfilling God's plans and purposes for their lives."[3] Simply defined, leadership is "a process whereby an individual influences a group of individuals to achieve a common goal."[4]

Leadership is not exercising power and authority to get people to do what you think they should do. In its purest form, leadership is influencing others to achieve a common goal. As a church leader, that common goal involves helping people grow. The common goal is not church growth; the common goal is the growth of people.

STYLES OF LEADERSHIP

Not only are there many different definitions for leadership, there are also many different styles of leadership. The following are a few of the most common styles of leadership.

LEADING GROWTH

Situational Leadership

Situational leadership is when the leader constantly adjusts his or her leadership depending on the situation. In this style of leadership the leader's behavior is closely linked with the follower's readiness. Situational leadership is about a leader's adaptability—whatever the situation calls for is what the leader seeks to become.

Transactional Leadership

Transactional leadership involves a transaction between leaders and followers. When followers fulfill expected duties and tasks, they are compensated for doing so (pay, bonuses, awards, etc.). When followers fail to meet set expectations they are punished (fired, demoted, ridiculed, reprimanded, etc.). Transactional leadership is based on bureaucratic authority and requires clear job descriptions so that followers will know exactly what is expected of them.

Charismatic Leadership

Charismatic leadership is when a leader exerts his or her influence over others through the power of personality to get others to do what they think should be done. Charismatic leaders use charm and charisma to attract followers, to make others feel good, happy, or excited about the organization, project, task, and so on. Charismatic leaders are energetic and enthusiastic. They know where they are headed, have great self-confidence, and are motivated by what they want to accomplish.

Participative Leadership

In the participative leadership style, leaders function as facilitators. Often used in corporate settings, participative leaders seek to facilitate discussion, ideas, and flow of information with the goal of arriving at the best decision possible. Although the participative leader is ultimately responsible for making the final decision, he or she will do so only after all considerations and factors that come from a collective group have been carefully considered.

Autocratic Leadership

In this command and control style of leadership, leaders function as the sole decision makers. Autocratic leaders make decisions without consulting team members, even though their input would have been useful. They expect rules and regulations to be followed, and immediate compliance is required. What the autocratic leader says goes and cannot be questioned.

Laissez-Faire Leadership

Leaders who lead with a laissez-faire style are aware of what's happening but largely refrain from getting involved. Instead, followers are given lots of freedom to do what they feel is best to do and how to do it. Laissez-faire leaders trust others to keep their word and fulfill their areas of responsibility. Such leaders offer support by supplying resources and advice but are not in any way controlling or micromanaging.

Transformational Leadership

The primary focus of transformational leaders is the organization. However, follower development and empowerment, although a secondary focus, are nonetheless crucial components in transformational leadership. Transformational leaders help others recognize and develop gifts, talents, and abilities and use such to make a positive impact on accomplishing the goals and purposes of the group or organization. Transformational leadership is not focused on maintaining status quo within a group or organization. Instead, they look to where the group or organization should be headed and determine what changes are needed to get there.

In that the primary focus of transformational leaders is the organization, much care is given to collaboration, teamwork, cooperation, and commitment to the overarching purpose of the group or organization. Transformational leaders understand their purpose is not to make every decision. Instead, through collaboration, a better method, vision, product, and so on can be achieved. Transformational leaders do this by treating others with dignity and respect, by placing great emphasis on alignment with the core values of the group or organization, and by appealing to others to transcend self-interest for the greater good.

Servant Leadership

Servant leadership has much in common with transformational leadership. Like transformational leaders, servant leaders help others recognize and develop gifts, talents and abilities. However, unlike transformational leaders, the primary purpose is the follower, not the organization. Servant leaders seek to take care of the needs of others before they take care of their own. Servant leaders serve the interests of their followers as opposed to forcing their own interests and wants on followers. Although servant leadership is heralded primarily among Christians, it has gained some ground within the marketplace. (Servant leadership is addressed more fully in chapter 7.)

PURPOSEFUL LEADERSHIP

These are just a few of the most popular leadership styles. But while there may be some value found in each leadership style, leadership that enhances growth involves more than choosing a particular leadership style from which to lead.

LEADERSHIP STYLES

Leadership is impacted by many factors that enhance growth, whether it is the growth of organizations, churches, or people. What might work well in one situation or circumstance may not work well in another. Leadership is not static; it is fluid. There is an ebb and flow to life, individually and organizationally. Likewise, there is an ebb and flow to leadership. Factors such as the life cycle of an organization, stages of group life, and so on can greatly impact leadership effectiveness. For example, the leadership style of a successful entrepreneur will not work well in mature organizations. Likewise, leadership that may work well in a mature organization will not be as effective in a start-up.

So how does a church leader lead effectively? This is a good question. But let me offer a better question. What is the overarching purpose of church leadership?

The purpose of church leadership is to equip others for their work of ministry. This is not to say that church leadership does not include other things such as financial matters, building needs, allotment of resources, and so on. But these other things, as important and as vital as they may be, are often the things that sidetrack church leadership from fulfilling their central calling—equipping others for their work of ministry. Unfortunately, many church leaders are so busy with everything else they are unable to fully engage in equipping others.

In contrast, church leaders who align with their purpose relinquish much of the control and responsibility they have been accustomed to. In doing so, others are given responsibility whereby they are able to fulfill their ministry. The result? Church leaders experience less stress and are enabled to function more fully in their calling—equipping others for their work of ministry. Instead of church leaders wearing multiple hats and carrying most of the load of ministry, church leaders are able to fulfill their God-given calling.

Many church leaders believe that as a leader they are responsible for making things happen. Thus, they believe in the need for strong leadership. Take control. Make it work. Make it go. This is especially true when dealing with "conflict, insufficient giving, lack of volunteers, flat attendance, lack of interest in missions, long-term members who leave, first-time visitors who don't come back, a decreasing number of baptisms," and so on.[5] But is an autocratic leadership style the solution to growing people?

The answer is obvious. Much of the work of ministry could be done away with by implementing one intentional strategy—equip others for their work of ministry. "There's a reason Christ modeled this method of ministry for us in the Gospels—it works!" Leaders who equip and empower others multiply their ministry. Leaders who don't equip and empower others carry the bulk of ministry alone or with a select few. Consequently, church growth is limited to the extent a church leader effectively equips and empowers others.

The key to effective leadership is not functioning in a particular style of leadership. The key is found in aligning oneself with the purpose of leadership. A good question to ask oneself is, "If my purpose is equipping others for the work of ministry, how might I lead in such a way to best enhance the growth of others?"

It has been suggested that "leaders equip followers by providing appropriate tools, equipment, and other resources so that the followers can be successful in their completion of assigned tasks."[6] But that is not all. Equipping others involves more than providing the necessary resources needed to accomplish tasks. Leaders equip others by encouraging, by teaching, by modeling expected behavior, by helping others discover their gifts, by creating and maintaining safe environments, by trusting others, by allowing others the freedom to make mistakes and to learn from those mistakes, and so on.

CONCLUSION

Jeff Jaco maintains the growth The Sanctuary has experienced is because of the commitment to grow people. When I shared with him what I wrote concerning his story (to make sure I had the correct details) this is what he said: "I have to tell you, as I read this last paragraph (when Jaco said he finally "got it") I just burst into tears while sitting in my recliner. That day changed my life as much as nearly any event I have experienced."

I believe you can have the same experience. When you finally "get it," when you decide that you will no longer strive to grow the church, but instead will focus on growing people, the very thing you have been desiring will happen. It may not happen immediately, and some may leave. But as Jesus demonstrated, when you invest in equipping and empowering others the result will be much greater than anything else you could do. Large crowds followed Jesus everywhere He went; that is, until they understood the ramifications of being His disciple. But Jesus never drew a crowd as large as what transpired through the equipping and empowering of others.

Through alignment with his Father's plan and purpose and servanthood, the movement Jesus founded transformed the world. I believe it can happen again. When we as church leaders align ourselves with our Father's plan and purpose—equipping others for their work of ministry—our world will be impacted in a greater way, much greater than it would have been if we were to merely try to grow churches.

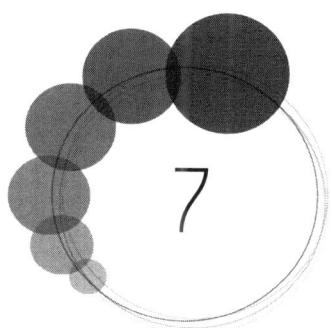

7

WHAT'S ALL THE HOOPLA ABOUT SERVANT LEADERSHIP?

THE MOST COMMON LEADERSHIP STYLE among Christians is servant leadership. In fact, it has become a buzzword. We hear it constantly—church leaders are to be servant leaders.

But what exactly does this mean? What is a servant leader? What does servant leadership entail? What does it look like? And most important, does servant leadership effectively help people grow?

The Bible has much to say about the concept of serving and servanthood. In fact, the word "servant" is mentioned over nine hundred times in the King James Version of the Bible, whereas the word "leader" appears only six times. Thus, much weight has been given, especially in recent years, to the concept of servant leadership—first servant and then leader.

Richard Krejcir, in "Servant Leadership Principles," states a servant leader is "someone who has the attitudes that Jesus had; who has been transformed by Christ; who places other's needs first; who has eternal values and God's timing in mind; who places integrity ahead of ambition; who sees glorifying Christ and serving Him as the measure of success."[1]

Krejcir continues describing servant leaders:[2]

- Servant leaders have His "basin and towel" attitude.
- Servant leaders do not neglect their family.
- Servant leaders are not weak—they are meek.
- Servant leaders think strategically.
- Servant leaders know how to lead themselves and others.
- Servant leaders are not willing to compromise truth to be more effective.
- Servant leaders should be able, while modeling the way, to get others to follow, and empower them to grow spiritually and in ministry.
- Servant leaders include the team in all major decisions and strategic planning for the ministry.
- Servant leaders work within their call, gifts, and Scripture.
- Servant leaders do not forget to support the church's overall vision and purpose statement, or place personal feelings higher or in place of it.
- Servant leaders know that loyalty, harmony, unity, trust, and commitment come from a collaboratively encouraging environment.
- Servant leaders listen to everyone, not just the ones in power or ones who have the influence.
- Servant leaders know that the effectiveness of their empowerment, training, and supervising of the team will determine the effectiveness of the ministry and church.
- Servant leaders can and should expect that Satan will not be happy with them, and must be aware of his various

ways of distraction and confusion, especially when success comes which infringes on his ground.
- Servant leaders will resist the latest fads and leadership trends that are unbiblical.

Although such things are noble, when reading through the list I can't help but wonder if servant leadership is truly a leadership style or just a buzzword.

Merriam-Webster Dictionary defines "hoopla" as "talk or writing that is designed to get people excited about and interested in something."[3] Is this what is happening? Is servant leadership talk just a bunch of hoopla or is there any substance to it?

SERVANT LEADERSHIP

Robert K. Greenleaf coined the phrase "servant leadership" in 1970, in a paper titled, "The Servant as Leader," in which he describes servant leadership as "servant first."[4] He states that servant leadership "begins with the natural feeling that one wants to serve, to serve first. Then conscious choice brings one to aspire to lead. That person is sharply different from one who is leader first, perhaps because of the need to assuage an unusual power drive or to acquire material possessions."[5]

Greenleaf suggests that if a person's first desire is to lead and secondarily to serve, that person is likely to have alternative motives, such as wanting power or possessions. In contrast, people who desire to be a servant first and then find themselves leading others is doing so for the right reason.

Greenleaf describes an important difference between servant leaders and those who are leaders first, an especially important difference for church leaders. He states,

> *The difference manifests itself in the care taken by the servant-first to make sure that other people's highest priority needs are being served. The best test, and difficult to administer, is: Do those served grow as persons? Do they, while being served, become healthier, wiser, freer, more autonomous, more likely themselves to become servants? And, what is the effect on the least privileged in society? Will they benefit or at least not be further deprived?[6]*

Unlike command and control leadership styles, which are commonly self-centered or self-focused, servant leaders are mostly interested in the growth and development of others. Rather than forcing people to do what they want, servant leaders serve their followers. Moreover, servant leaders believe that "organizational goals will be achieved on a long-term basis only by first facilitating the growth, development, and general well-being of the individuals who comprise the organization."[7]

WHY YOU SHOULD WANT TO BE A SERVANT LEADER

There are many reasons why Christian leaders should want to serve others. The main one is because serving others is what Jesus did and what Jesus instructed others to do. As in other teachings of Christ, His instruction regarding serving others was countercultural. Derek Tidal, in "Leaders as Servants," says that during the first century leadership was "masculine, powerful and concerned with status. It was dedicated to accomplishing the task, no matter what the cost to ordinary people. But Christ introduced a new way of leading which was to be incumbent on all his followers, that of leading by serving, even sacrificial service."[8]

Christ not only spoke about leading differently, He also demonstrated it. Jesus washed His disciples' feet. He then told them, "I have given you an example, that you should do as I have done to you" (John 13:15). In other words, serve others. Through serving you will lead.

The apostle Paul did the same thing: he taught leaders to lead by serving. And not only did he teach it, he demonstrated it in how he led others. Although Paul referred to himself as an apostle, teacher, and other things, he mostly described himself as a servant, slave, or household steward.[9] Paul, in a detailed description of himself in I Corinthians 3:5–4:13, emphasized his lowly status and unimportance.

Throughout Scripture Paul repeatedly referred to himself as a colleague rather than a superior. In Romans 16:9, Paul said, "Greet Urbanus, our fellow worker in Christ." In Romans 16:21, he referred to Timothy as "my fellow worker." In addressing the church of Corinth Paul said, "For we are God's fellow workers" (I Corinthians 3:9). In II Corinthians 8:23, he referred to Titus as "my partner and fellow worker." In Philippians 2:25, Paul called Epaphroditus a "fellow worker and fellow soldier." These are just a few verses of Scripture that showcase Paul's view of himself. There are many more.

In addition to Paul's comments regarding being a servant, Peter taught that leaders are to be servants "in a way that obviously echoes the teaching of Jesus (I Peter 5:1–4). They are shepherds who must not lord it over their flocks and must remember they are accountable themselves to the Chief Shepherd."[10]

Unlike Paul, many church leaders do everything but refer to others as fellow laborers. Instead, others are commonly referred to as "my people," or "my saints." Is this merely a byproduct of church culture? Or is this a deeper issue, one that is rooted in a leadership philosophy in which leaders believe that people exist to serve the leader, rather than the leader to serve the people?

Unfortunately, many "leaders are concerned about title, status, position and the honor they are due."[11] They are quick to take offense and to defend their honor, but not Paul. Paul was not concerned about many of the things we are concerned about. In fact, "Words for honor are significantly absent in any discussion of leadership in Paul's writings."[12]

THE TENSION IN SERVANT LEADERSHIP

In spite of the great support for servant leadership found in Scripture, the servant leadership style is not without its critics, especially when it comes to putting it into practice. Sometimes what may sound good on paper does not always work well in reality. And some think this is true regarding servant leadership, at least in some aspects.

For example, there is the authority issue. Some maintain that servant leadership can lead to a minimization of the authority of leaders. When a servant leader caters to the needs of others, people will be less likely to view the leader as an authoritative figure. And without this authority leaders will not be able to lead others effectively.

Another issue that receives pushback involves the demotivation of followers. If the servant leader is constantly trying to fix things, always taking care of things, it may cause followers to believe the leader will meet or fulfill all the needs that may arise. Consequently, the people who are being served by the leader will sit back and do little or nothing to help. After all, what is the purpose of getting involved if the servant leader is going to do it?

The tension felt in servant leadership also involves the element of vision. Although there are great benefits in allowing others to be a part of a process in which vision is crafted, there are times when leaders must lead the way, and at times do so alone. There are times when a leader needs to explore new opportunities, brainstorm ideas, formulate a new picture of where things are going, and needs separation from followers to be able to do so.

WHAT'S ALL THE HOOPLA ABOUT SERVANT LEADERSHIP?

Which causes one to ask, "How can one simultaneously be a leader and a servant? Are not the roles of leader and servant irreconcilable? Do they not call for opposing abilities and characteristics? Are they not more readily in conflict with each other than in harmony?"[13]

The tension in servant leadership is witnessed among Jesus' disciples. Jesus' teaching concerning servant leaders was contrary to their concept of leadership. The disciples were trying to figure out who was going to get which leadership position; Jesus was trying to get them to see the importance of serving.

This problem still exists today, even among church leaders. Many church leaders believe "leaders command and servants obey; leaders determine the direction and servants follow. Leaders supply vision and strategic thinking; servants deal with the mundane and everyday. Leaders are proactive; servants are reactive."[14] But this is not what Jesus was trying to teach His disciples about leadership; it is the complete opposite.

And yet the tension remains. In theory, servant leadership sounds great. But in reality is it practical?

So here is the question—how can a church leader accomplish things while constantly serving, especially if the church leader is the pastor? Tidal states,

> *The tension is a very real one for many pastors who daily seek to practice servant leadership, often putting themselves under some degree of stress as they do so. Trained to preach, teach and lead in mission, many pastors end up putting out the chairs, dealing with the plumber and locking up the church—more caretaker than pastor. Seeking to avoid the constant worry of being able to affirm that they are both leading and serving, some resolve the tension by emphasizing one pole at the expense of the other.*[15]

The tension is very real for some pastors. Some pastors find themselves striving to meet every need of others. "They will often find themselves undertaking menial tasks and putting themselves out to keep the flock contented and, as much as possible, united."[16] Some pastors constantly find that "the pace of any change is often set by the slowest of the sheep and great attention is shown to the stragglers in the flock."[17]

Subsequently, the question regarding servant leadership becomes, is this a proper understanding of servant leadership? Is this what Jesus had in mind when He taught His disciples to lead by serving? Additionally, when Christians speak of servant leadership, do they know what they are talking about? Is servant leadership something just to talk about, or is it something we actually are supposed to do? Is servant leadership a valid form of leadership? Or is it just something leaders call for others to live by, while they personally adhere to other forms of leadership, such as command and control styles of leadership in which others serve them, not in which they serve others?

RECONCILING LEADERSHIP AND SERVANTHOOD

Although the word "leader" appears only six times in the King James Version of the Bible, it would be wrong to assume the Bible does not talk about leadership. Indeed, there is a great amount of attention given to leaders and leadership within the Bible.

Tidal states, "The form and focus of leadership varies over time. The Patriarchs give way to the tribal leaders who then acknowledge the authority of Moses, the exceptional leader, and his heir Joshua, and who are then followed by Judges who summon the tribes as a whole to fight for deliverance from oppression."[18]

"Throughout the Old Testament the picture becomes clear, leadership is essential if any society is to be healthy."[19] The fall of man can be viewed as a lack of leadership on the part of Adam. The children

WHAT'S ALL THE HOOPLA ABOUT SERVANT LEADERSHIP?

of Israel coming out of Egypt were in need of a leader. In Numbers 27:16–17, Moses pleaded with God, "Let the Lord, the God of the spirits of all flesh, set a man over the congregation, who may go out before them and go in before them, who may lead them out and bring them in, that the congregation of the Lord may not be like sheep which have no shepherd."

Likewise, the Book of Judges showcases the need for leadership—without it, chaos reigns and weakness is displayed. Furthermore, the books of the Major Prophets and Minor Prophets suggest the need for someone to lead and to lead properly.

The New Testament also expresses a value for leadership, howbeit, much through the act of serving. Paul is a prime example. The apostle Paul's leadership was not hierarchical in nature; his role as a leader was functional. He sought to grow others, to empower others, and thus to eliminate as much as possible the dependence of others on leaders. In other words, Paul, by the nature of his calling, had power and authority, but used it in the form of serving with the objective of developing others. He did not use his power and authority to cause people to depend on him and to serve him and his purposes. And yet Paul was clearly a leader.

Paul's leadership emulated that of Christ's leadership, who, in many ways, sought to deconstruct hierarchical leadership. Jesus declared in Matthew 28:18, "All authority has been given to Me in heaven and on earth." But in John 4:34, He stated, "My food is to do the will of Him who sent Me, and to finish His work." Likewise, in John 5:19, He said, "The Son can do nothing of Himself, but what He sees the Father do." And in John 6:38, Jesus declared, "For I have come down from heaven, not to do My own will, but the will of Him who sent Me." Moreover, in John 8:28, Jesus stated, "I do nothing of Myself."

Thus, Jesus, who has been given all authority, subjected His authority to fulfilling the will of the Father. He "humbled Himself and became obedient to the point of death, even the death of the cross" (Philippians 2:8). The one who was given all authority "was crucified in weakness" (II Corinthians 13:4). He embraced the cross. He died to all self-seeking, self-glorification, and self-will.

Most people who talk about servant leadership use Jesus as a model. But most fail to reference His ultimate sacrifice, which was the sacrifice Jesus made by not using His power for personal gain. Jesus restrained Himself from the use of power for personal advantage. He subjected Himself to the overarching purpose—the Father's will.

It is from this basis that the tension in servant leadership is obviated. Power is kept in check when used for a higher purpose—the growth, the well-being, and the empowerment of others. This is what we as church leaders must strive for.

Tidal states,

> To be authentic, Christian leaders have to embody these alternative values and demonstrate their message in the manner of their leadership. The use of power is subordinate to the goal of empowerment. Placed in this context, the idea that leadership means power over others disappears and the tensions between leadership and servanthood evaporate.[20]

Paul had little difficulty reconciling leadership and service. He expressed much of his power and authority as a leader in terms of parental authority. He referred to himself as a father who had several sons. Moreover, "he use[d] a Jewish form of parental authority to govern the churches he [had] founded while also acting as their servant. So, although he could command and on occasions did, he would prefer to persuade."[21]

In addition, Paul, as a father figure, "was not above working manually, undertaking voluntary and self-imposed disciplines, and suffering many, humiliating hardships for the sake of his children."[22] His self-sacrificing ways were what one would expect of any father or mother. "From one angle, fathers are the leader of the family, but from another angle they are quintessentially servants."[23]

Sadly, this is often missing among many church leaders. Some leaders who freely use the word "servant" are in fact "tyrants, dictators, self-aggrandizers, and benevolent oppressors."[24] This should not be.

The tension in servant leadership is real and must be addressed. It is not enough to speak servant leadership language and then lead others in ways that do not express servanthood. The focus of church leadership must be on equipping others for the work of ministry. The motive of church leaders should not be to direct the activities of others. Instead, it should be to motivate, influence, inspire, and empower people to focus on ways to serve others.

TRANSFORMATIONAL LEADERSHIP

Although church leaders serve others, in serving others they must never lose sight of the higher purpose, which is alignment with God's plan and design for the fivefold ministry. Thus, church leaders ultimately serve the King.

Back in the days of the Wild West, the sheriff served the people. But his serving the people was not subject to the desires of the people; rather it was for the overall good of the people. For example, there were times in which the sheriff withstood lynch mobs even when it was unpopular to do so. Although the people demanded the release of a prisoner so they could take justice into their own hands, the sheriff stood against their wishes, knowing it was for the overall good of the community even though it meant going against their wishes.

Leadership is not giving in to the desires of the people when the desires of the people are harmful to the people. In fact, leadership has been defined from time to time as influencing people to do things they would not do otherwise. Such understanding is best applied in multiple scenarios. For example, a leader who constantly steps into situations to solve problems may be keeping people from learning and growing. Likewise, leaders who do not let others fail, to make mistakes, do the same. Leaders who constantly implement rules and regulations and fail to teach principles also hurt the growth and development of people.

A leadership style very similar to servant leadership is transformational leadership. "Both transformational leadership and servant leadership emphasize the importance of appreciating and valuing people, listening, mentoring or teaching, and empowering followers."[25] Like servant leadership, transformational leaders help people grow. They strive to move followers to "go beyond their own self-interests," to give themselves to the greater good of an organization, group, or community.[26] Unlike servant leadership, however, the underlying motive is not the individual; it is the purpose of the organization. Thus, in the case of church leaders this means a church leader not only helps people grow but leads people to help others grow as well.

CONCLUSION

This is the ultimate motive of Jesus' discipling the disciples: that they in turn would disciple others. Thus, Jesus not only displayed the characteristics of a servant leader, He also was a transformational leader in that He was aligned with the purpose of the spread of the kingdom of God and sought to disciple others to align themselves with the same purpose.

Although Jesus exemplified servant leadership, it would be a misrepresentation to say that was the only style of leadership Jesus emulated. Consequently, in our desire to fulfill our calling—equipping others for their work of ministry—we would do well not only to serve others, but to call for others to in turn serve others. In doing so, our motivation will not be to others as much as it will be to alignment with the overarching purpose of making disciples who make disciples. And this is the way it should be.

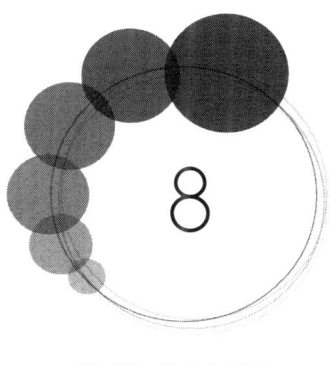

8

GROWTH ACTIVITIES

IT IS NAÏVE TO THINK one can make someone else grow or make anything grow, for that matter. Growth does not happen that way. But that is not to say leaders cannot do things to enhance growth or increase the possibility of growth. Unfortunately, some leaders do not understand how this works. Instead of leading growth, they attempt to force it. This should not be.

WHAT HIGH-PERFORMING EXECUTIVES DO

So how does a leader enhance growth? What exactly do effective leaders do?

Harvard professor and *New York Times* best-selling author, John Kotter, decided to find out what effective leaders do. Over a period of several months he shadowed fifteen high-performing executives, interviewed them, and talked to their subordinates. What he ended up with was a look into how leaders spend their time, how they lead, and the patterns behind what they do. Kotter discovered that successful general managers (GMs) usually conform to the following patterns:[1]

- *They spend most of their time with others.* The average GM spends only 25 percent of his working time alone, and this is spent largely at home, on airplanes, or while commuting. Few spend less than 70 percent of their time with others, and some spend up to 90 percent of their work time this way.
- *The people they spend time with include many in addition to their direct subordinates and their bosses.* They regularly see people who may appear to be unimportant outsiders.
- *The breadth of topics in their discussions is extremely wide.* GMs do not limit their focus to planning, business strategy, staffing, and other top-management concerns. They discuss virtually anything and everything even remotely associated with their businesses.
- *GMs typically ask a lot of questions.* In a half-hour conversation, some will ask literally hundreds.
- *During these conversations, the GMs rarely seem to make "big" decisions.*
- *Their discussions usually contain a considerable amount of joking and kidding and often concern topics that are not related to work.* The humor is often about others in the organization or industry. Non-work discussions are usually about people's families and hobbies.
- *In more than a few of these encounters, the issue discussed is relatively unimportant to the business or organization.* GMs regularly engage in activities that even they regard as a waste of time.
- *In these encounters, the executives rarely give orders in a traditional sense.*
- *GMs often react to others' initiatives; much of the typical GMs' day is unplanned.* Even GMs who have a heavy schedule of

planned meetings end up spending a lot of time on topics that are not on the official agenda.
- *GMs spend most of their time with others in short, disjointed conversations.* Discussion for a single question or issue rarely lasts more than ten minutes. It is not at all unusual for a general manager to cover ten unrelated topics in a five-minute conversation.
- *GMs frequently engage in attempts to influence others.* However, instead of telling people what to do, they ask, request, cajole, persuade, and intimidate.
- *They work long hours.* The average GM studied works just under 60 hours per week. Although GMs can do some of their work at home, while commuting to work, or while traveling, they spend most of their time at their places of work.

Interestingly, what high performing GMs actually do is not what most people would imagine. Most people think such leaders would be controlling, demanding, or given to performing. But then again, most people are not high-performing leaders. Perhaps this is why. Most people don't do the things high-performing leaders do.

WHAT JESUS DID

There are many leaders I admire, men who have influenced my own leadership and concepts of leadership. I admire the writings and leadership insights of people like John Maxwell, Andy Stanley, Jim Collins, and Patrick Lencioni. Leaders such as my father, father-in-law, pastors, bosses, educators, and so on have impacted me. I love the subject of leadership and have been a student of it for many years.

LEADING GROWTH

The greatest impact any one individual has had on leadership, however, is Jesus. Jesus' leadership style is still impacting the world today. Notice the following things Jesus did:[2]

- *Jesus was willing to invest in people others would have dismissed.* Consider the disciples. They were not the "religious" elite, yet Jesus used them to start His church.
- *Jesus released responsibility and ownership of ministry.* Consider how Jesus sent the disciples out on their own. No micro-management, it appears.
- *Jesus had a leadership succession plan.* Jesus consistently reminded the disciples that He wouldn't always be with them. Of course, He was still the "leader", but He left others to take the ministry forward.
- *Jesus practiced servant leadership better than anyone.* The King of kings was willing to wash the feet of His followers.
- *Jesus was laser focused on His vision.* Regardless of the persecutions or distractions, Jesus kept on the mission God had called Him to complete.
- *Jesus handled distractions with grace.* When the woman who had been bleeding for 12 years touched His garment, Jesus stopped to heal her, even though He was headed to a definite purpose.
- *Jesus was into self-development.* Jesus constantly slipped away to spend time with God.
- *Jesus was into leadership development and replacement.* He very purposefully prepared the disciples to take over the ministry. He pushed people beyond what they felt they were capable of doing.
- *Jesus held followers to high expectations.* Jesus was not afraid to make huge requests of people. "Follow Me,"

meant the disciples had to drop their agenda to do so. He told the disciples they must be willing to lose everything to follow Him.

- *Jesus cared more about people than about rules and regulations.* He was willing to jeopardize Himself personally by breaking the "rules" to help someone in need.
- *Jesus celebrated success in ministry.* He rewarded people generously who were faithful to Him and His cause.
- *Jesus finished well.* Any questions whether His ministry was effective? Still working today.

SIMPLE THINGS LEADERS OF GROWTH DO

What I find simple yet striking is the similarity concerning the activities of effective GMs and those of Jesus. Both are centered on people; both are concerned with growth—of people and self; and both are deeply committed to leading. Also, both understand leadership is not something that occurs in isolation. Leadership takes place within the context of others. Leadership is the process by which a person influences others toward a common goal.

Some leaders are in love with the vision they have for the future. They are ambitious and driven to accomplish something of importance, to experience success. While on one hand a person might argue these are good traits—after all, a lazy leader will not accomplish much of anything—on the other hand a leader with vision must be careful not to force the vision on others. Why? Because the goal is not accomplishing a task; the goal is changing the lives of people. And no one wants to be forced into things. While one might manage things, people must be led. "It may be a bit cliché, but at the end of the day, followers are human beings. Don't lose sight of that reality."[3]

LEADING GROWTH

Hence the following activities of a leader are not tasks, per se; rather they are ways in which a leader influences others toward the common goal—disciples making disciples.

Teach

Jesus clearly stated His teaching consisted of what He had seen the Father do and heard the Father say. Such is the nature of learning. People learn both by hearing and seeing as well as doing.

Teaching is not just giving instruction, telling someone what to do. Teaching involves modeling what is said, or what could be called "learning through observation" (Matthew 28:20). It is not about the transfer of knowledge; it is about people becoming. This is why it is so important for teachers to first "become," because what a person becomes will impact what a person does. Any dichotomy between what a teacher says and what a teacher does is false and unbiblical.

In that teaching involves modeling the expected behavior, teaching must extend beyond the confines of church buildings. It is outside the pulpit where others can best see lessons taught in action. Although church leaders may not personally be able to teach all people in this manner, church leaders must take time to invest in the equipping of team members by spending time with them. This is the pattern of leadership development displayed by Jesus. Much of the training and development of the twelve disciples occurred outside of formal instruction "in a 'field-type,' real-life learning situation."[4]

Leaders, especially when developing leaders, should view themselves as facilitators of the learning experience. For example, leaders who create and maintain a learning environment, an environment in which penetrating questions are welcomed, help facilitate learning. In an interview with *TIME*, Eric Schmidt, CEO of Google, said, "We run this company on questions, not answers." Schmidt understands that questions enable a person, group, or organization to gain understanding. Likewise, Jesus, the ultimate teacher, welcomed questions. He also asked them. In fact, Jesus asked a total of three hundred and seven questions.[5] "Jesus' use of questions "made people think for themselves and examine their hearts."[6] His use of questions helped stimulate learning, as can be seen in Peter's disclosure of Jesus' identity. (See Mark 8:27–29.)

Motivate

The days of commanding commitment from others are nearing an end. "You can push weak, needy, or fragile people into conformity. But, once you push someone, you have to keep pushing. Conformity isn't commitment."[7] Instead of commanding people to commit to growth, leaders should seek to motivate people.

Neither should leaders manipulate people to commit to growth. While incentives may motivate some to commit, the commitment will only be as good as the incentive, and will last only as long as the incentive lasts. Additionally, the commitment will only be as deep as the incentive.

Many leaders do not know how to motivate others beyond the use of incentives and a stick (command and control). But there is a better way. When it comes to motivation, contemporary science points to three universal psychological needs: autonomy, relatedness, and competence.[8] Leaders who meet these needs stand the best chance at motivating others to commit to growth.

"Autonomy is people's need to perceive that they have choices, that what they are doing is of their own volition, and that they are the source of their own actions."[9] Remarkably, "the way leaders frame information and situations either promotes the likelihood that a person will perceive autonomy or undermines it."[10] Leaders who view themselves as team members will do much better at promoting autonomy than those who act like an owner of a team.

"Relatedness is people's need to care about and be cared about by others, to feel connected to others without concerns about ulterior motives, and to feel that they are contributing to something greater than themselves."[11] As church leaders, we have a great opportunity to help connect people to a deeper meaning of life, a deeper purpose. This is what relatedness is about—connecting what people do to a noble purpose.

And competence is about people feeling effective in meeting challenges as well as opportunities. It is about being able to demonstrate skill. It is also about having a sense of growth. Leaders can help people feel competent not only by teaching them but also by encouraging them and by maintaining a learning environment.

In order to motivate others, leaders must shift their focus from "What can I give people to motivate them?" to "How can I facilitate people's satisfaction of autonomy, relatedness, and competence?" While other forms of motivation may work for a period of time, sustained peak performance occurs when people act because they want to, not because they feel they have to. "The issue is their motivation, not yours. Speak to their values, drives, and questions. You don't convince. They convince themselves."[12]

Invite

Leaders of growth invite others to connect on an emotional level. Connecting with others is about "sincere interest in and concern for others, a heightened ability to listen to people, and a strong capacity to clearly understand different viewpoints."[13] Connecting with others requires a leader to respect others, including the opinions, concerns, and worldviews of others.

Leaders who invite others to connect on an emotional level understand the role of communication in connecting, that it is not a one-way street. Connecting on an emotional level requires followers to speak up. It also requires leaders to listen and listen well. People become frustrated when they feel they are not being heard, and being heard involves more than mere transference of information. It involves connecting on an emotional level. For this to happen leaders must invite others to share what they are thinking. Furthermore, leaders must take action concerning things discussed. If no action is taken, people will begin to feel frustrated.

Internal frustration is one of the signs of an unhealthy team or church. This is what was happening in Acts 6. Internal frustration threatened to thwart the momentum of the early church. However, because the people were invited to share, because the apostles connected on an emotional level, the problem dissipated.

Church leaders must be cognizant of the fact that respectful people will not voice their thoughts if they do not feel their thoughts are wanted. In addition, most people will refrain from sharing if they feel they will be rejected or looked down upon. This can be a real challenge for church leaders in particular. Michael Michalko states, "Any controlling authority, no matter how carefully presented, will tend to inhibit the free play of thought. If one person is used to having his or her view prevail because he or she is the most senior person present, that privilege must be surrendered in advance."[14]

Last, leadership that is controlling is seldom inspiring or inviting. Emphasizing duties and rules does little to help people grow. While it may enforce compliance, it will not help people become the change. While it may generate immediate results, it has little longevity. Again, the goal is not performance; the goal is to equip people.

Share

The goal of a church leader is not to do ministry for people, but rather to do ministry with people. For this to happen church leaders must share ministry. That is, church leaders must allow others to perform ministry. Church leaders cannot perform most of the work of ministry and expect others to grow. And much of the growth of others occurs while sharing in ministry.

In order for sharing of ministry to occur, leaders must be willing to trust others with ministry. Most commonly, the challenge in trusting others is the perceived possibility of a lesser quality of ministry. Thus, church leaders must ask, "Is the possibility of a lesser quality of ministry more important than the growth and development of the one performing the ministry?" Church leaders must also consider the message being sent to the entire congregation—is it one in which performance is valued or learning valued? Leaders who desire to equip others will not allow the desire for quality to supersede the desire to align with purpose—equipping others for their work of ministry.

Sharing in ministry will at times involve sharing pertinent information with others. Leaders will not share information if they do not trust the one with whom they are sharing the information. But trust cannot be developed unless leaders are first willing to extend trust.

In many situations, much more than what most leaders recognize, the trust that is needed for ministry to function fully is lacking. Rarely will people say aloud, "I do not trust you." However, the lack of trust most often is communicated through actions such as excluding others from activities, not sharing meaningful information, and not following through on commitments. Tension or stress in a relationship is also a sign of a lack of trust. Additionally, the lack of morale within a group is often a byproduct of a low level of trust, as are rumors, gossip, and constant questioning of decisions of leadership.

As one might expect, such an environment in which there is a low level of trust is an environment in which people will not be able to grow to their fullest capacity. In contrast, an environment in which there is a high level of trust is one in which leaders are not afraid to admit mistakes, are willing to share information crucial to the success of others, are in constant communication—never leaving followers second-guessing what a leader might be thinking—follow through on commitments, and behave in a trustworthy manner. Additionally, in an environment in which there is a high level of trust, leaders take upon themselves the responsibility to generate trust, understanding that when both parties trust one another sharing of ministry can occur.

Last, church leaders must understand that when inviting others to participate, especially other leaders, the desire to share in ministry will be particularly strong. If such leaders are constantly kept in the dark on matters of importance, are not appreciated, continually encounter a lack of communication, and so on, such leaders will eventually leave. And the problem in most situations is not a bad attitude or spirit. Rather, it is failure on the part of church leaders to communicate, to share, and to invite the upcoming leader to participate to his or her fullest capacity. Unfortunately, "many churches are willing to embrace shepherds, teachers, and pastors . . . but they're unwilling to embrace leaders."[15]

Qualify

C. Gene Wilkes, in *Jesus on Leadership*, maintains that developing others for ministry involves qualifying them, and suggests that this development requires upholding high standards of discipleship.[16] Although doing so may eliminate some, this should not deter church leaders from upholding high standards of discipleship.

Wilkes makes the point that large crowds of people followed Jesus, and then states, "Most church leaders would see this as a good thing" and would find a way to let everyone know.[17] "Jesus, on the other hand, knew that most of those following had no clue what following him actually meant."[18] Jesus told the crowd, "If anyone comes to me and does not hate his father and mother, his wife and children, his brothers and sister—yes, even his own life—he cannot be my disciple." (See Luke 14:26.) This was certainly not a seeker-sensitive approach. Jesus was clear about the cost of discipleship. He knew it would cost something.

However, qualifying consists of more than just upholding high standards of discipleship; it involves mentoring and teaching, training and developing. Qualifying others involves equipping others to fulfill ministry. Wilkes refers to Paul's qualifying Timothy:

> Paul was Timothy's mentor. Paul equipped Timothy as they traveled together (Acts 16:1-5). When Paul felt Timothy was qualified to do ministry without him, he left Timothy in Ephesus to lead the church (I Timothy 1:3). Paul later wrote to the young pastor and told him to entrust what he learned from Paul to faithful men who would also "be qualified to teach others (II Timothy 2:2). Qualified in the verse means to be fit or competent for something. Paul told Timothy to find "reliable," or faithful, men whom he could train to teach others.[19]

Qualifying others is still a vital aspect of helping others grow. Moreover, leaders must qualify others so that others may qualify others.

Empower

In some ways, empowerment has become a buzzword. Leaders talk about wanting others to take ownership but few are willing to empower others. Some talk about empowerment, but in actual practice, do nothing of the sort. Instead, they simply delegate. The fact is, leaders can talk about empowerment but their talk is gibberish unless people believe it's safe to act without permission.

GROWTH ACTIVITIES

Empowering others does not do away with the need for delegation. There are times in which delegating tasks and responsibilities to others is needed. However, there are also times in which people need to be empowered.

Leaders who want to make sure things work as well and as effectively as possible face a temptation to hoard power and authority. But when core leaders retain control, they limit the growth of others. Additionally, the danger with core leadership hoarding control is that "people become resources to be developed rather than human beings . . . who are encouraged to choose and shape their own future."[20]

Church leaders often talk about the leadership of Paul and seek to lead like him. But some mistake Paul's approach to leadership. Paul did not lord over people. Instead, Paul sought to develop people and to empower those whom he helped to develop. His goal was not to receive the credit as the one-and-only leader of the people; Paul's goal was to empower others to carry out the gospel. His goal was to release ministry, to share ministry, to let others take up the mantle.

Empowering others does not mean that the one who does the empowering no longer has anything to do. Leaders who empower others have the responsibility of articulating the overarching vision, reminding people of the overarching vision, and calling people into alignment with the core values of an organization.

A clear vision is an absolute necessity when empowering others. Empowerment without a clear vision will almost certainly result in chaos. People must be able to connect with the big picture; they must know where they fit in. Empowerment isn't permission to do whatever a person wants; empowerment is collaborative, not isolated. Empowerment is the permission to act in ways beneficial on behalf of the overarching vision and purpose, to do what one ought to do. It is permission to act within the core values of the organization.

CONCLUSION

In this chapter we have addressed leadership activities that enhance growth. In doing so, we have considered a few key aspects of a leader who helps others grow. Now ask yourself, "Am I this type of leader? What do my actions say about my leadership style?"

Ask yourself the following questions to see if you are an equipper. Look for any areas in which you might need to grow—that is, if you want to become a leader who best helps others grow.

- Do I have a clear understanding of my purpose as a church leader?
- Am I aligned with my purpose?
- Do I have a biblical definition of success?
- Are my goals as a leader centered on the growth of others?
- Do I spend adequate time with my team?
- Do I invest much effort in encouraging others?
- Does the team I work with possess the competence, abilities, and skills necessary to equip others?
- Does our team understand and appreciate differences in gifts and personalities of one another?
- Do I share leadership or desire to remain in control?
- Do I highly value the opinions of others?
- Do I regularly invite others to offer their input?
- Am I primarily focused on achieving what I want to achieve?
- Do I extend trust to others?
- Do I seek first to listen, then to share? Or do I expect others to do the bulk of listening?
- Have I created an environment that helps others grow, or do I just tell others how to grow?

- Do team members have the necessary resources, supplies, and support needed?
- Do team members constantly have to ask for the things they need?
- Do team members feel appreciated?
- Can others make mistakes and learn from them without my holding it over them?
- Are others encouraged to challenge the process?

The mindset, values, and practices of a leader who helps others grow are counter to the typical leadership style of many church leaders. However, equipping others, helping others grow, is what we are called to do. And thus we must seek to adhere to the mindset, values, and practices described in this chapter—that is, if we are going to grow others and subsequently experience church growth God's way.

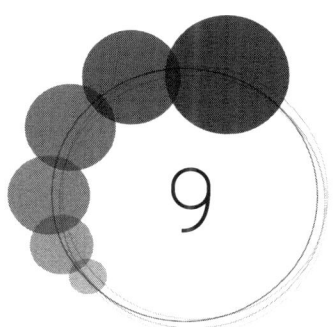

9

IS ACCOUNTABILITY EFFECTIVE?

THERE IS A BELIEF that accountability is a necessary element in the development of others, especially leaders. For example, I have heard some say, "Accountability is essential if you are going to receive a double portion of anointing." And, "If you are accountable to the one you follow, you will receive their anointing upon your ministry." And, "Everyone needs an apostle to whom they are accountable." But is this what the Bible teaches regarding accountability? Is accountability a vital aspect in leadership development? Does it help others develop, to become equipped for ministry?

It also is a fairly common belief that in order to get things done—to accomplish tasks, to experience collective growth—holding people accountable to duties, tasks, responsibilities, and so on is a must. Hence, should leaders expect others to be accountable to them so that God's mission on the earth might be accomplished? Is holding people accountable to commitments, tasks, duties, and responsibilities a necessary and effective means to getting things done around the church?

GOOD AND BAD ACCOUNTABILITY

Scripture supports the idea of accountability. Proverbs 27:17 states, "As iron sharpens iron, so a man sharpens the countenance of his friend." While taking assessment of my life some years ago, I noticed much of my talk was of a negative nature. I imagined if I were to continue along the same path I would eventually become a cynical and skeptical person. Not liking this, I sought a different path. Along with destroying sermon notes in which I pointed out the negative in order to support the positive, I asked my wife and a few close friends to confront me when hearing me speak negativity. They did. I changed. And I am a better person because of it.

There have been other times when I have experienced iron-sharpening-iron accountability, times in which I initiated the conversation by asking friends and elders to help improve me and times in which friends and elders initiated the process. There also have been occasions in which I was the one doing the sharpening. Such encouragement and support among friends is a crucial element in a person's growth and development. In this way, accountability is of immense benefit.

Another Scripture passage in support of accountability is Hebrews 10:24–25: "And let us consider one another in order to stir up love and good works, not forsaking the assembling of ourselves together, as is the manner of some, but exhorting one another, and so much the more as you see the Day approaching." The writer of Hebrews encourages us to consider one another, to stir up love and good works, not to forsake getting together. Such factors are crucial in the life of a Christian and can be seen as accountability.

Yet another supportive verse of Scripture for accountability is James 5:16: "Confess your trespasses to one another, and pray for one another, that you may be healed. The effective, fervent prayer of a righteous man avails much." Here again we see the interconnectedness of the body of Christ. No one is an island to himself. Confessing to one another and praying for one another is instrumental for healing. In fact, based on the words of James, it can be derived that one of the reasons some lack healing is due to the lack of what could be termed as accountability.

Thus accountability can help people grow. And it can be beneficial in helping people overcome sin. Having someone you can talk with, confide in, and confess to can be of great value.

But as with most everything, the practice of accountability can be taken too far. Some have taken the concept of accountability and applied it in ways contrary to the teachings of Scripture. For example, there is a huge difference in a person asking someone to hold them accountable concerning a specific matter, welcoming others to speak into one's life, and being commanded to be accountable to a specific person.

Also, accountability can be harmful in that it can give a false sense of growth—if a person is accountable and answers some specific questions, it is easy to believe he or she is experiencing growth. But this is not always true. Some seek accountability with others as a way of dodging deeper issues. This is not good and does nothing to help a person experience growth. And some turn accountability into a program or a specific process in which it is closely monitored rather than allowing it to be organic, something that stems naturally from a relationship. Hence, accountability can offer value, yet it also can be detrimental to the very thing it is supposed to do—help people grow. It depends on how it is applied; it depends largely on the philosophies of leadership.

WHY HOLD PEOPLE ACCOUNTABLE?

Many leaders advocate the use of accountability to make sure people accomplish tasks, meet expectations, and fulfill responsibilities.

The question these leaders need to answer is this: "Why do you need to hold people accountable in the first place?"

Susan Fowler, in "If You Are Holding People Accountable, Something Is Wrong (And it isn't what you think)," asks,

> *If you believe people need to be held accountable, what is your underlying belief? Is it that people cannot be trusted to do what you want them to do? Is it that people fail to follow through on what they commit to do? Why is that? Is it because they are lazy and irresponsible—or worse, intend to do harm? How did you come to believe people cannot be trusted?*[1]

Fowler continues, "Have you had an experience that caused you to believe that, given the chance, most people cheat, lie, and steal? Do you have proof to substantiate your belief that people will miss deadlines, fail to achieve their goals, and slack off if you don't keep your eye on them?"[2]

Interestingly, in spite of how some leaders think, the evidence does not point to the need for accountability as a means of getting people to follow through in their areas of responsibility. Instead, the overwhelming evidence is that people want to contribute. Most people are willing to work hard and feel good when they do. And most people want to achieve common goals and are excited when they do so.

So why aren't people as engaged as they should or could be? W. Edwards Deming, widely considered the father of the quality movement in the United States and Japan, claims that 80 percent of nonperformance is most likely due to system failures.[3] Research supports Deming's assertion: "Distributive injustice (unfair allocation of resources) and procedural injustice (unfair or secretive decision-

IS ACCOUNTABILITY EFFECTIVE?

making and processes) are the two primary reasons for a lack of work passion in employees.[4]

Don't miss this. The number one reason for nonperformance is because people perceive injustice in the distribution of resources (for example, finances) and unfair or secretive decision-making and processes. Unfortunately, many church leaders just don't get it. They think the problem is that people are aloof, don't care, have a low level of commitment, and so on. But such things are seldom the problem. The problem is usually a breakdown in leadership. The number one cause for a low level of passion is that followers don't trust the leader. Yet leaders continue to function from faulty beliefs that are based on faulty assumptions, such as the problem is people. Yes, sometimes it is. But more often than not, the problem is one of leadership.

If you are thinking, *I have proof that people will fail to perform if they are not held accountable,* it may still be the fault of leadership. Let's consider special giving and evangelistic efforts. A typical approach taken by many church leaders is to use incentives to get people to give, to get people involved in evangelism.

"The problem is that leaders don't understand the undermining and short-term effect of carrots, so when those bribes don't work, leaders assume it is the individual's fault and put accountability measures—the stick—in place."[5] Do you see the problem with this? "The insidious thing about accountability is that it promotes the use of pressure to get people to do what they probably already want to do—succeed."[6] Thus, "The only traditional motivation technique more undermining than a carrot to activating optimal motivation is the stick."[7] And yet this is a common approach taken by many leaders. Many have a "you ought to" approach rather than a "how to" approach, which is somewhat surprising when considering the equipping nature of the fivefold ministry.

PHILOSOPHY IMPACTS ACCOUNTABILITY

Again, as has been previously suggested throughout this book, a leader's philosophies will impact how a leader leads. When you hold the belief that church growth is the purpose, you are likely to overemphasize results. You are apt to resort to pressure to get people involved in activities that will increase attendance. You may even be tempted to employ unethical practices. When given a choice, you might choose short-term results over long-term results.

One factor that appears to have a great influence on a leader's concept of accountability is the leader's relationship with his father. Many leaders who demand accountability from others either have or have had a less than ideal relationship with their father. Typically, the leader's father was either abusive or absent during the leader's childhood. In contrast, those who have healthy relationships with their fathers—one in which the father treats the mother with love and respect, does not provoke his children, and is respected in his household not because he demands it, but rather because he earned it—seem to have a better understanding that accountability is a natural byproduct of relationships. Such leaders understand that accountability does not have to be mandated; it is something that is reciprocal—the son is accountable to his father and the father is accountable to his family. Accountability is not a one-way dynamic; it's a two-way dynamic.

Think about your leadership style. What is the real purpose of accountability? Is there a better way to accomplish what needs to be accomplished? Is there a better way that might help a person grow, develop, and become equipped? How might your decisions and actions as a leader be different if you no longer believed your responsibility as a leader involved holding people accountable?

"Accountability works better when it is experienced in a constructive way than when it is imposed in an inquisition-like mode."[8] So consider how an alternative belief would generate a different approach to your leadership. How would your decisions and actions be different if you were to truly align with your calling of equipping others for their work of ministry?

People will either live up or down to your expectations of them. If you constantly treat them as though there must be accountability or nothing will get accomplished—as though you do not trust them— they will not trust you. In contrast, if your approach is one in which you are an equipper you will show people "how to," and consequently, people will live up to your expectations and many will exceed them. Imagine the difference it will make when people start living up to your high expectations instead of hovering under your low ones.

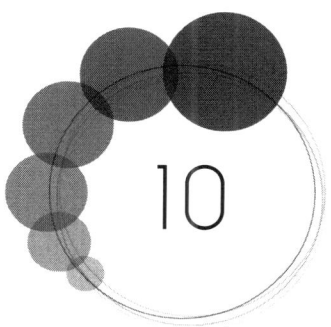

STRATEGIC THINKING FOR GROWTH

SEVERAL YEARS AGO, a church where one of my friends serves as pastor experienced a tremendous revival. In just a few months, over one hundred people were added to the church. Unfortunately, one year later not one person who was added during that season of growth remained. When I asked him to what he credited the growth of the church, he responded, "I do not know. I only know one thing—we were not prepared for it." Thus the church was unable to sustain growth.

What happened with my pastor friend is not uncommon. It is one thing to experience growth; it is another to sustain growth. What I can't figure out is why so many church leaders place an enormous amount of emphasis on growing (revivals, evangelism efforts, etc.) but so little emphasis on sustaining growth. Similarly, many emphasize conversion (getting people saved), but put little effort, in comparison, toward helping people grow in their walk with God, to discover their ministry, and equip and empower them to fulfill their ministry.

Such leadership showcases the lack of strategic thinking that goes on in many churches. This chapter addresses the need for church leaders to participate in strategic thinking, especially when it comes to growth, and in particular, the growth of people.

FIVE GROWTH PRINCIPLES

Before looking more deeply into strategic thinking, let us consider a few growth principles as they pertain to individuals:[1]

Growth principle number one: Growth is possible.

Anyone and everyone can experience spiritual growth. The size of church does not determine whether or not a person experiences growth. People can grow in small churches; people can grow in large churches. Church size does not determine whether or not growth is possible. Neither does what a church may or may not have to offer in ways of programs and specialized ministry determine whether or not growth is possible. Anyone and everyone can grow.

Growth principle number two: People are responsible for their growth.

Ultimately, the responsibility of growth lies upon individuals. Church leaders are not responsible for people growing. Yes, church leaders are to help people grow. They are to equip people. They are called to develop others for the work of ministry. Thus, church leaders encourage, teach, instruct, model, and so on, but church leaders are not personally responsible for the growth of individuals. The responsibility lies upon the people.

Growth principle number three: Growth occurs best in community.

The growth of people cannot be sustained long term outside of a relationship with others. That is, it is impossible for a person to experience sustained growth when failing to participate in meaningful relationships with other believers. Iron sharpens iron. This is the method Jesus used when discipling His disciples. Much of the personal growth of the disciples took place within the context of a group. People who want to grow want to spend time with others who want to grow. Thus, church leaders need to create forums and/or give opportunity for meaningful relationships to develop among church members, especially those who are new to the church. One of the ways churches can do this is through ministries of service. Churches need to look for ways for people to get involved in serving, with the purpose of relationship building.

Growth principle number four: Developing a person's desire for growth is key.

It is impossible to make a person grow. You can, however, create environments in which people are encouraged to grow, environments in which many people become excited about growth. When people understand that growth is possible and learn how to grow, engaging in growth becomes exciting. Thus, stories of life change should be shared everywhere and often. When people see how others are growing, they will want to grow.

Growth principle number five: The goal is to help people achieve growth.

The goal is to introduce people to Christ, to teach them truths of faith, to help them discover their calling and gifting, and to empower them to fulfill their ministry.

STRATEGY

There are additional principles of growth that can be shared and much more that can be stated. These principles, however, are foundational to a proper understanding of the importance of a strategy as well as the role strategic thinking fulfills in creating that strategy.

Strategy is commonly defined as a plan. But that is not entirely accurate. A better definition is that "strategy is a pattern"; it is what actually takes place over an extended period of time.[2] Therefore, it could be stated that your strategy for growth is not your plan for growth; it is what you do, or have done, over a period of time regarding growth.

Some people do not like to plan, but that does not mean they do not have a strategy. It simply means that their strategy is to fly by the seat of their britches. Others develop plans but do little to implement or follow the plan. And others develop a strategy and implement it.

Many church leaders are notorious for putting together a strategy and getting excited about it. But putting together a strategy is only a small part of things. The strategy must be implemented, and this is where the real work of a strategy comes into being. It is one thing to craft a plan; it is another to work the plan; it is yet another to participate in strategic thinking when crafting a plan.

The need for a well-defined strategy is paramount. Churches and church leaders who fail to develop a strategy for growth are prone to becoming too inwardly focused. In addition, they will almost always place too much focus on events as opposed to processes. Why? It is because events do not require sustained effort. And the results of an event can be quickly realized and easily measured for those who believe the success of an event is determined by how many people show up. Thus it is easier to get excited about an event than it is to get excited about a process.

STRATEGIC THINKING FOR GROWTH

STRATEGY AND DISCIPLESHIP

What is your strategy for helping people grow? Can you articulate it? Does your leadership team know what it is? Is the environment of your church a learning environment? Are you, as well as others in the church, actively engaged in personal development? If so, you are leading by example and helping to create a learning environment. If not, you may be sending the message that you have arrived and that personal development is not important.

Let's suppose you are intent on growing people. Do people know what the pathway for growth is? Are church members helping others walk that pathway? Do newcomers know what the next step is in their developmental process? Is the pathway of assimilation and discipleship for new believers clear, or are people left to figure it out for themselves? What is being done to help people discover their gifts, callings, and place to serve?

These questions and others like them should cause church leaders to consider their strategies for helping people grow. Are the strategies effective? Church leaders should ask themselves, "Are we working the strategy or are we allowing other things to get in the way of what we are called to do—equip people for the work of ministry?"

Ron Edmondson states, "Knowing that people are responsible for their growth, and that I can only create environments where that can best happen, helps shape where I spend my efforts in discipleship."[3] Edmonson touches two crucial elements in a strategy for helping others grow—environments and what we as church leaders choose to do with our time and resources. Are we giving due diligence to creating an environment for growth? And what are we choosing to spend our efforts and time on? The answers to these questions help us to identify our actual strategy.

So where does one start? When it comes to identifying and crafting a strategy for helping people grow, what should be the focus? I suggest the first step should involve defining what an authentic disciple looks like. What does it consist of? I would also suggest that the definition should include, among other things, the fact that a disciple makes disciples. If people are not actively engaged in ministry that helps to make disciples of others, it is doubtful they are authentic disciples. Discipleship consists of more than a class, more than an event, more than being faithful with church attendance, and so on. Real disciples impact the lives of others; real disciples affect environments with biblical values and truths. Thus, a strategy for helping people grow must be concerned with more than measuring success based on quantity; it must consider quality.

Second, the strategy should include a process that can be implemented in moving people from believers to disciples. This is a huge challenge for many church leaders, as many are given to events and programs rather than systems and processes. Consequently, many add activities to the church calendar, hoping that people will get involved. And some will use incentives (manipulation) or a stick (coercion) to try get people to attend church services/activities, believing church services/activities best help people grow. However, "churches that are seeing a dramatic increase in the spiritual climate of the congregation have shifted their focus away from activity for its own sake to intentionality. People aren't looking for something else to do; they are looking for something to do that matters!"[4]

Thus, an effective strategy for growing people must not only include what to do, but also what not to do. This is a real dilemma for many church leaders. Too many are like an octopus on roller skates—there's a tremendous amount of activity, but the octopus is going nowhere in particular. This should not be. Surely this is not God's intention.

Church leaders need to evaluate the relationship between existing programs and the strategy for helping people grow. It may be that some activities and programs may need to be eliminated. Too often churches do things simply because they have been doing them for a long time. Leaders must stop and ask, "Is this beneficial to helping people grow? Is it effective? Is there a better way of doing things?" Church leaders must ask the tough questions and not be afraid of the answers. In addition, they must develop a strategy to implement changes, if needed.

Are you effectively impacting the growth of people? If so, the people you lead are giving, attending, telling others about Christ, volunteering, and serving. You are not wondering what to do to get people involved in ministry. Instead, you have an abundance of volunteer leaders who are looking for a place to serve. In addition, if people are growing, their stories will be numerous. If, on the other hand, "you can't find any stories to tell, you probably don't have an effective equipping strategy."[5]

STRATEGY AND LEADERSHIP DEVELOPMENT

Research shows that more than 70 percent of employees do not feel appreciated or valued by their employers.[6] Consequently, it is of little surprise that more than 30 percent of employees believe they will be working someplace else within the next twelve months. Hence, Mike Myatt, in his article "10 Reasons Your Top Talent Will Leave You," maintains, "Employees who are challenged, engaged, valued, and rewarded (emotionally, intellectually and financially) rarely leave, and more importantly, they perform at very high levels."

Myatt notes that smart leaders don't make the following mistakes. Here are his ten reasons why top talent leaves:[7]

1. Failure to unleash their potential
2. Failure to challenge their intellect
3. Failure to engage their creativity
4. Failure to develop their skills

5. Failure to give them a voice
6. Failure to care
7. Failure to lead
8. Failure to recognize their contributions
9. Failure to increase their responsibility
10. Failure to keep your commitments

Myatt states, "Bottom line, if leaders spent less time trying to retain people, and more time trying to understand them, care for them, invest in them, and lead them well, the retention thing would take care of itself."[8]

Although Myatt's article deals with the marketplace, it has tremendous value when applied within the context of the church. If leaders spent less time trying to retain leaders, and more time trying to understand leaders, care for leaders, invest in leaders, and lead leaders well, the retention thing would take care of itself.[9] Hence, a well-developed strategy for leadership development consists of such matters.

The common strategy for leadership development consists of monthly leadership meetings and yearly leadership retreats in which generic leadership principles are taught. While there is certainly benefit in such an approach, if this is the extent of the strategy, it will lack some essential components in the developing of leaders.

Effective leadership development must extend beyond classroom instruction; it must consist of more than the sharing of basic leadership principles. As Jesus demonstrated with development of the Twelve, some things are better caught than taught. This is not to say that instruction is not important. But investing in the development of others must extend beyond instruction.

In recent years the idea of mentorship has skyrocketed. But high-capacity leaders are usually quite busy and do not have time to take part in what many are looking for in a mentoring relationship. Thus, asking someone to be mentor or agreeing to mentor someone who is asking you to mentor him or her seldom works. What does work is organic mentoring. That is, simply spending time with others, talking and sharing insights, thoughts, cares, concerns, and so on. When people know you care about them and are willing to invest time with them, especially informal times, it can make a great impression. An additional benefit is that "people who have experienced this tend to keep the cycle going, and it builds a culture of leadership development."[10]

Thus, the most effective leadership development flows from a culture of learning. Leaders can help build a culture of leadership development by sending team members to conferences, by buying and giving away leadership books, by hosting leadership retreats, and so on. But the benefit of such things will most likely not be the event itself or the book or the instruction; rather it will be that leadership was willing and even eager to invest in others. People appreciate and are impacted when they know you care about their development. Again, such actions help build a culture of leadership development.

Another factor beneficial to developing leaders is allowing them opportunities to put into action the skills they are learning. One of the most frustrating things for a person is to feel he or she has something to contribute but is not allowed to do so. Church leaders need to be especially aware of leaders who feel they have outgrown their position or area of responsibility but are unable to identify a place for advancement. If the vision is too small, this will happen often. And up-and-coming leaders will be left with the choice of becoming stagnated in their current position/areas of responsibility or leaving to go elsewhere.

A culture of leadership development should permeate the entire church; this includes children's ministry, student ministry, worship ministry, and so on. It is not limited to those who are typically considered a leader. The leadership potential of a church is less when church leaders fail to invest in leadership development across all spectrums of church ministry. A culture of leadership attracts volunteers. It helps people identify their gifting, equips them in their gifting, and allows them to minister within their gifting.

Last, church leaders are not the only people who can influence a culture of leadership. Many church leaders are fearful of doing so, but

> there may be an assistant principal, coach, bank president, or corporate executive who is further along the leadership pathway than anyone else in your church. Some of these people are experienced, high capacity leaders with great potential to train future volunteers. Calling on their experience can go a long way in building a culture of leadership.[11]

STRATEGY AND VISION

When I say that leaders need to share the vision with others, people tend to think this means leaders need to articulate vision in such a way that others are able to understand it. While there certainly are times when this is true, this is not what I am saying. I am saying that leaders need to share ownership of the vision. And at times this will involve allowing others to be a part of helping to create the vision.

Unfortunately, many leaders do not share the vision or give the vision away. Instead,

> leaders often operate out of fear and hold too tightly to their vision, afraid others will ruin their "dream", but this never allows people to develop, stifles growth, and doesn't allow the body (or

the organization) to perform at its best. Ultimately it keeps the leader's vision from achieving maximum potential.[12]

By holding on to vision, by not inviting others to have a voice in crafting the vision, leaders miss a wonderful opportunity in the growing and development of others. In addition, failure to give the vision away results in a low level of buy-in from others. If others do not feel they own the vision, they will not be committed to the fulfillment of the vision, at least not as much as the leader is committed. But many leaders do not believe this. Instead, they believe the problem is that they did a poor job in communicating the vision. Hence, church leaders often look for new and more effective ways to state the vision. But this is seldom the problem. The problem is usually a failure on the part of leaders to give the vision away.

How do leaders give the vision away? How do they allow others to own the vision as though it is theirs? The key is in finding people whom you can trust to take the vision and implement it with their personal touch while you stay out of their way and let them do their job. Many times the end result will be that the vision will end up looking much different than it did at first. However, it will be much better than it would have been if you were the only one who owned it.

STRATEGY AND STRUCTURE

The Welsh revival broke out in November 1904. Within two months of its beginning, there were over 30,000 converts, and within six months, 100,000 people experienced conversion. The impact was felt across the nation. Support for national sports dissolved. Theaters were empty. Taverns closed. Crime dropped. Brothels and gambling dens were invaded. Businesses closed during lunch as people fasted and prayed. But just a few years later it was as though nothing happened. Why?

One possible reason for the lack of sustained revival was the lack of structure. Services were spontaneous and unorganized. People did solely whatever they felt led to do. Evan Roberts, the leading figure of the Welsh Revival, stated, "I have been asked concerning my methods. I have none. I never prepare the words I shall speak."[13]

In contrast, William Booth, who visited the Welsh Revival, was highly structured. Booth, a British Methodist preacher, founded the Salvation Army with the purpose of getting people saved. Unlike the Welsh Revival, which ended shortly after it began, the Salvation Army remains. However, today it shows little resemblance of its original purpose, which could possibly be contributed to its heavy emphasis on structure.

Similarly, some have too much structure; others do not have enough. Structure can either help or hinder leaders as well as churches. It is overbearing when it does not accommodate the rise of leaders, stifles creativity, and causes people to go through too much red tape to get things done. On the other hand, structure is lacking when no one knows what is going on, chaos is the norm, and there is a lack of consistency even in the smallest of matters.

The type of structure any organization maintains has a substantial impact on the type of followers it retains. Horizontal structures encourage followers to become partners, to actively participate in the decision-making, to share opinions, to be involved in creativity. Other structures, such as hierarchies, do not.

Most organizational structures are hierarchies, as are most churches. Hierarchies consist of rules, procedures, and regulations. In hierarchy-structured organizations, followers are expected to do what the leader says. They are not to question leaders, share their opinions, or ask leaders for help in clarifying why things are as they are.

Traditional forms of organizational design, such as hierarchies, involve "breaking tasks down to their smallest components, defining jobs as narrowly as possible, then exerting tight structural and managerial control."[14] Sadly, this describes many ministries. Such forms of organizational design do not release people; they control people. Thus, they are not conducive to helping people grow or to developing leaders. Instead, they foster "authoritarianism and its destructive offspring; distrust, dishonesty, territoriality, toadying, and fear."[15]

Church leaders must take a close look at structures and analyze whether or not they are conducive for growing people as well as growing leaders. If they are not, church leaders must be willing to make changes. Creating structures that allow people to get involved, to have a voice, to have ownership of the vision will go a long way toward gaining buy-in crucial to the fulfillment of the vision.

One way to make constructive changes to organizational structure is to empower the people that matter and allow them to participate in changes to the organizational structure. Forward movement often "comes through process and structure changes that are part of a common vision of the people—people with energy, commitment, and a sense of ownership of the new reality."[16] Success occurs when all parties involved are able to contribute.

Some might resist this approach, and refer to it as democratic rule; but that is inaccurate. Involving others is how the apostles addressed the crisis in Acts 6. By allowing others to have a voice, the situation that might have derailed the early church became a huge win. Sadly, many church leaders miss out on such moments because of failure to empower people. This is not to say that church structure should be one in which people rule. But neither should it be one in which church leadership rules.

STRATEGY AND STRATEGIC THINKING

Most strategies are limiting because the basis has a small view or perspective of things. This is because most strategies do not include strategic thinking; most strategies are crafted from strategic planning. There is a difference.

Strategic planning is one in which forecasting, not foresight, is used to make plans. Usually this involves such things as looking at last year's calendar to see what was done last year, and then looking at next year's calendar to identify a date for the event or program. Hence, strategic planning is static; once the strategy has been crafted it does not change. This is why the same event or program is usually repeated year after year with little thought given as to whether or not the event or program is accomplishing the overarching purpose of the church.

When church leaders approach strategizing from a strategic planning perspective, they are prone to first make plans and then strategize how to make the plan become a reality. But what if the initial plan is faulty? What if there was a better objective worth pursuing? Strategic planning does not concern itself with such. Unfortunately, this is how most people strategize. When crafting a strategy, most leaders participate in strategic planning.

Few leaders accurately assess how the decisions they make impact things on multiple levels. The reason is because strategic decisions usually are made by a single individual or with a select few. In contrast, strategic thinking strives to see the big picture. Thus, leaders who engage in strategic thinking will look to see things from the peripheral. They will engage in collaboration; they will welcome the thoughts and opinions of others.

Whereas the focus of strategic planning is on the creation of the plan as the ultimate objective, strategic thinking sees the planning process itself as a critical value-adding element in which others are able to contribute and be impacted. Strategic thinking strives to see the underlying connections and interactions that might otherwise be missed.

Unfortunately, most church leaders will go to great lengths to plan a special event but stop short of connecting the event to an overarching process that connects one event to another event. For example, many churches will do something special to create an event that draws a crowd but fail to plan a follow-up event for new guests to connect with others in meaningful relationships. Similarly, many churches place great emphasis on what occurs in the altar but do little to connect people to a pathway of discipleship. There are many examples from which I can draw concerning the lack of strategic thinking within churches. I see it everywhere. Few leaders engage in strategic thinking; most engage in strategic planning.

So how might a church leader engage in strategic thinking to enhance the growth of people? Consider the following trends and some possibilities that might help others experience growth:[17]

Online as the new default

A new platform in which leaders can influence others is the online platform. Have you participated in any strategic thinking regarding it? If your response is a moderately outdated website, podcast, or Facebook page, you are barely scratching the surface. One of my friends recently told me of a church that has discipleship classes online for those who cannot attend the classes in person; church services are recorded and archived with printable PDF handouts; webinar training and leadership meetings; and so on.

Wi-Fi and smartphones

Have you participated in any strategic thinking concerning Wi-Fi and smartphones? People are looking up the Greek meaning to words, Scripture verses, commentaries, and the like, and checking out other options while listening to your sermon. *"Do you assume your audience is intelligent, literate and has options?"*[18] What can you do to enhance *the growth of people through such tools? Have you considered having conversations with people on the peripheral to get their opinions and insights? You might be surprised at what could be generated if you did.*

Dialogue

Dialogue is a trend that is having a great impact on churches in spite of the fact that many leaders are clueless of it. "People want to talk, not just listen. While sitting around tables every Sunday may not be the answer, increasingly a church without conversation is a church without converts."[19] Have you participated in strategic thinking as to how this trend will continue to impact the church? Are you looking into venues in which you can foster the need for conversation—both online and in person?

Lack of guilt

It used to be that guilt was a motivating factor in getting people to do what leaders thought people should do. Those days no longer exist. This is a trend that affects the approach of many leaders. How will such leaders adjust? Will they continue to operate with a style that is no longer effective, or will they look to do things a little differently? The ability to participate in strategic thinking will impact their ability to adjust accordingly.

Declining trust in authority

The level of trust for authority continues to decline, as does the level of respect. This is not to say that people will not trust; but trust will have to be earned. People no longer start out trusting; they start out with suspicion. How you exercise authority will largely determine people's respect and trust in you. Have you considered this trend and adjusted accordingly? Or do you maintain that people should respect and trust you because you are a man of God? If so, you might find it increasingly difficult to be a leader that enhances growth.

Declining trust in institutions

How about the declining trust in institutions? Forty years ago, four out of five top global brands were nonexistent.[20] How might this impact the way people view the church, a 2,000-year-old institution? Strategic thinking considers such a trend; strategic planning does not. For example, strategic thinking would consider the declining trust in institutions in how it does children's ministry. Are background checks made for children's workers? Do guests feel their child will be well taken care of and safe in your care? What are you doing to identify possible changes needed?

Declining trust in media

It used to be that people trusted mass media such as news telecast, radio, and so on, but not any longer. For example, nowadays only 47 percent of people trust television ads.[21] In contrast, 70 percent of people trust online consumer reviews, up 15 percent since 2008, and "92 percent of people trust recommendations from friends and family above all other forms of advertising, up 18 percent since 2007."[22] How might this trend of a declining trust in media impact things?

CONCLUSION

The temptation for leaders is to ignore trends, to pretend they don't exist, to think they will not impact ministry, to continue doing things the way they have always been done. But such trends (there are many more) present the church with wonderful opportunities for ministry perhaps a little different than the past, but marvelous opportunities nonetheless.

LEADING GROWTH

What are you doing to consider such things? How might you involve others in creating a robust strategy, one which is generated through strategic thinking? Remember, growth principle number one: growth is possible. And principle number five is, the goal is to help people achieve growth. The goal is not to hold on to outdated methods; the goal is to help people grow.

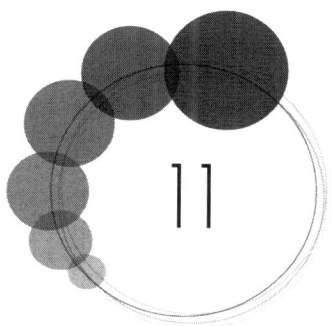

11

GROW YOURSELF

ASK YOURSELF THE FOLLOWING QUESTIONS:[1]

- Do you spend adequate time with your family?
- Do you regularly develop and equip others?
- Do you try to be too much to too many?
- Do you have unrealistic expectations of yourself as well as others?
- Do you say no to yourself so that others can do ministry?
- Do you have a system of time management and do you abide by it?
- Do you regularly take time off?
- Do you take care of your physical body?
- Do you have a good system to calendar and keep track of events and dates?
- Do you spend adequate time with our Lord?

Your answers to these questions give insight to whether or not you are a healthy leader. Healthy leaders live balanced lives and influence others to do the same. Leaders who are unhealthy do not.

Unfortunately, many leaders are unhealthy. For example, consider the following: Seventy percent of pastors constantly fight depression.[2] Eighty percent say they have insufficient time with their spouse.[3] Eighty percent of pastors feel unqualified and discouraged in their role as pastor.[4] Fifty percent are so discouraged they would leave the ministry if they could but have no other way of making a living.[5] And fifteen hundred pastors leave the ministry each month.[6]

Over and over again, research suggests that the majority of leaders are unhealthy. And these are the very people trying to help others grow. Clearly, for this to happen, these same leaders must embrace growth. This is not to say that leaders must be perfect; that is not a reality. However, they must be deeply committed to pursuing personal growth. Not doing so would be a disservice to the very people leaders are trying to lead as well as to themselves. There is no other way around it. It is impossible to be a leader of growth and not grow personally.

EIGHT QUALITIES OF HEALTHY LEADERS

Thankfully, most leaders want to grow, and those who do will find the following eight qualities of healthy leaders to be of value. If any of these qualities are missing, leaders will struggle helping others to grow. Here are the eight qualities:

They maintain self-awareness

Healthy leaders are aware of what is going on inside of them. They do not ignore signs of tiredness, discouragement, or depression. Unlike Elijah, who experienced mental and physical exhaustion and prayed that God would let him die, healthy leaders are aware of when they are reaching their limit physically, mentally, and emotionally. If a leader does not maintain self-awareness, he or she will be clueless of any need for growth.

Healthy leaders are not afraid to explore their emotions; they are aware of what makes them feel sad, afraid, and angry. They understand how past experiences, hurts, and upbringing impact their thought patterns, concepts, and philosophies. Moreover, healthy leaders are aware of how such things might impact their decisions as well as relationships with others. Consequently, they are not blind to how their inward world might impact the lives of others.

They have a right philosophy regarding priorities

Healthy church leaders have an understanding that their relationship with God, spouse, and family is of greater priority than ministry. Furthermore, they have the philosophy that one of the greatest impacts their ministry makes actually stems from their marriage and home life. This is what Paul was addressing in his leadership qualifications in I Timothy 3. When a leader places greater priority on his ministry at the expense of spouse and family, not only does he cause damage to his spouse and family, he hurts his efforts in helping others grow.

In contrast, unhealthy leaders

> *view their marriage as an essential and stable foundation for something more important—the building of an effective ministry, which is their first priority. As a result, they invest the best of their time and energy in becoming better equipped as a leader, and invest very little in cultivating a great marriage that reveals Jesus' love to the world.*[7]

Unfortunately, too many church leaders have a faulty philosophy regarding priorities. Such leaders need to grow. The cost of not growing is too high a price to pay.

They seldom overextend themselves

"Emotionally unhealthy leaders are chronically overextended."[8] They seldom have time to focus on the things they should do because they overextend themselves by agreeing to too many other things.

> *If you were to ask them to list their top three priorities for how they spend their time as a leader, it's unlikely that cultivating a deep, transformative relationship with Jesus would even make the list. As a result, fragmentation and depletion constitute the "normal" condition for their lives and their leadership.*[9]

In contrast, healthy leaders refrain from committing to things just because it is an opportunity. Healthy leaders seek to discern God's will and to align with it. Furthermore, healthy leaders do not resist solitude. They embrace it. Also, they do not consider solitude and silence a luxury, but rather a necessity to being a healthy leader.

They regularly participate in rest and renewal

Healthy leaders participate in rest and renewal. Like Jesus, they understand the importance of withdrawing themselves for times of refreshing. They do not allow opportunities to determine activity; neither are they governed by the needs of others. Healthy leaders practice Sabbath rest in which they cease from all work.

Church leaders often struggle with regular times of rest and renewal, especially bi-vocational leaders. Knowing that so much needs to be done is a driving factor with many who struggle to take a break. However, much like tithing, in which we trust God to make up the difference, healthy leaders who practice the Sabbath trust God with the things they are unable to accomplish. Healthy leaders understand work will never be completed; therefore, they will regularly take time to rest in the midst of work. Thereby, such leaders experience renewal for the long haul.

They think big picture

Healthy leaders think big picture. They are not trying to accomplish everything right now in a single message or service, in one counseling session, and so on. They understand it is a journey, that some things take time. Furthermore, they are content with it being a journey and even find joy in the journey.

Healthy leaders think big picture for the organization. They understand the concept of a team—everyone working together for the overall good. They understand the decisions and actions they make have a far greater reach than self. They appreciate and are concerned about what is occurring on the peripheral. Additionally, healthy leaders, in thinking big picture, resist the building of silos within organizations. They know that silos create small-mindedness within others when the church is to be a collective body.

They release control

Healthy leaders release control; they are not trying to do it all themselves. Furthermore, when releasing control they do not take it back when others do things a little differently than they would have done them. Healthy leaders are growing leaders, and as such, help grow others. By releasing control, others can experience growth. In contrast, unhealthy leaders do not release control. Consequently, unhealthy leaders struggle to help others grow.

They embrace diversity

Healthy leaders celebrate diversity. By valuing diversity, healthy leaders are able to build healthy teams. They don't try to force others to be like them, to do things the way they would do them, to say things the way they would say them. Healthy leaders understand that through diversity people of all types can be impacted. Thus, healthy leaders welcome diversity on the team. They do not want yes-men in their inner circle; they want men and women who have an opinion and are not afraid to share it.

They pursue personal growth

Healthy leaders never feel they have arrived. They understand the importance of constantly reaching forward while at the same time being content with the process. Thus, healthy leaders are given to pursing health. Healthy leaders understand that becoming is more important than doing.

HOW TO BECOME A HEALTHY LEADER

Did you find any areas in which you are lacking? Areas in which you are presently growing or have recently experienced growth? If so, you are in good company. No one leader has arrived; all leaders should embrace growth.

The following four areas are crucial in the ongoing pursuit of personal growth; leaders who lack any one of the four will struggle with participating in ongoing growth. Here are the four areas:

Focus

Most leaders will struggle from time to time with staying focused. Day in and day out, leaders are involved in multiple areas of responsibility, constantly juggling things, hoping they don't drop anything, and all the while fighting against distractions that contend for their attention. Thus, the challenge with focus is very real and very important.

It is virtually impossible to escape distractions, and increasingly so in today's world of technology. Furthermore, due to the fact that church work involves people it is impossible to plan for everything that may occur.

Hence, considering the vast array of activities and distractions leaders encounter, there is a need for a system by which leaders can function. Leaders without a system are highly susceptible to distractions and prone to spending their time taking care of urgent matters, even though they may not be important matters. And this happens all too often in the lives of leaders. Things that matter but are not urgent (like personal growth and development) do not receive adequate attention.

Not long ago, I became overwhelmed with things—so much to do, so little time and resources with which to do them. I was struggling with focus, unsure of what needed my attention, jumping from one activity to another and making little progress with anything. A new season of my life was presenting me with challenges that my old system by which I functioned was unable to accommodate. I needed help.

Thankfully, a new friend entered my life. He serves as a leadership coach and organizational consultant, and is especially gifted with start-ups. In a short period of time, he helped me craft a plan of action that freed my mind so I could concentrate on matters at hand. No longer was I preoccupied with trying to juggle everything; instead, I was able to trust my system. The increase in energy has been amazing. I no longer feel overwhelmed with things, even though my list has gotten larger. My new system is more than able to handle it. I have shared it with others and have seen it work for them too.

The system is simple, and designed to be as such. In fact, whenever it starts getting complicated, things are headed in the wrong the direction. I have tried various task management apps. And while each of them offers some benefit, I have discovered that such things do not mean a person has a system by which they function. Many just have a cool task management app. That is all. The key, therefore, is not the app but the simplicity of the system and then working the system.

Here is a short synopsis of the system: Make a list of everything you said you were going to do, want to do, thought you might do, agreed to do, and so on. This list should consist of the things that are important to you, things that you think about often, things that keep cropping up in your mind. Typically, the average person will have just a little less than one hundred items on his list.

Once the list is formed, carefully consider each item. Is it something you are going to do? Is it something you are going to defer to a later time? Is it something you are going to delegate? Or is it something you are going to delete?

Now look at your to-do list. The things you can do in a few minutes, go ahead and do them. The sooner you have them completed the more your mind will be able to focus on other things. Now consider the things you are going to do that will require more than a few minutes. These items will usually require multiple steps of action. Next, try to identify "like" items. That is, items that would tend to belong to the same overarching purpose or project. Group these items together. This typically results in approximately ten to fifteen different and distinct groups.

The next step is to create a "desired outcome" for each of the groupings. This is your vision for the future in relationship to this specific area. The desired outcome is a crucial element often missing in many task management resources. It serves as a reminder of the purpose and helps to keep you focused.

Once the desired outcome has been created, create a next step for each group. Determine what you are going to do within the next week in order to begin moving forward. Don't make the next step so large that you are unable to accomplish it. Keep it simple. The key is forward progress, not immediate accomplishment.

Last, schedule time in your calendar to work on the next step. And, while allowing some flexibility, do your best to work your calendar. In other words, let your calendar drive much of what you do. If God can give you a message to preach days before you preach it, surely He can guide you in scheduling your calendar.

While I have shared only a small part of the system with you, even in its entirety the system is simple. We often overcomplicate things, and consequently end up wasting time and making little progress. The key is to have a system that frees your mind so you can focus on the task at hand. This is what the system is designed to do.

My friend has helped leaders of all types of organizations with this simple yet highly effective system. And now I am helping others. I know from personal experience its effectiveness, and have seen it work with individuals as well as organizations.

We tend to overload our minds. Consequently, we start forgetting things we would not typically forget. We struggle to fall asleep because we can't get our minds to stop working overtime. We struggle with alleviating stress from our lives. And it is mostly because we lack a system by which we function.

Leaders of growth understand the importance of a quality system by which they function. It is a crucial aspect in the ongoing growth of most leaders.

Boundaries

Leaders often overextend themselves and get involved in areas they should not because they want to feel important, needed, valued, and validated. Recently, I had a pastoral friend, who is viewed by others as having achieved great success, tell me he constantly overcommitted and overextended himself because of a personal need he has with wanting to feel needed. He also admitted that at times his family suffered because of this.

He is not alone. I have seen other church leaders do the same thing. These leaders need to learn how to set and maintain boundaries. I had to learn this and am still learning.

A boundary is a fence to ward off potential problems and to protect those in its guardianship. When we establish the right boundaries in our lives, our ministries do not suffer. They actually will be more effective. For example, what good does it do for a church leader to continually break commitments to his family in order take emergency phone calls and set up emergency meetings to help couples who are experiencing marriage difficulties? If a church leader does not set boundaries, such as no phone calls during supper time, or schedule "emergency" meetings at a time that does not break prior commitments to his wife or family, in time his own family will suffer. Of course, there are occasional exceptions, but the allowance of occasional exceptions should never be allowed to become the norm.

This is not to say that church leaders should be like hermits. Church leaders are in the people business. Boundaries just help to create the balance that is needed. Leaders must train other leaders to help respond to needs within the congregation, and then they must release them to do so. The church must be taught that the pastor does not have to make every hospital call; others can help carry the load of ministry. The pastor does not have to be the primary caregiver. Others can be included. The pastor is called to be an equipper. He is not called to be a one-man show. When the pastor tries to do it all, it robs others from being able to fulfill the ministry God has called them to. Furthermore, others will likely be able to do the job better than you anyway. How is this so? It is likely to be their primary calling. It is not yours. Your primary calling is to equip others.

In order for boundaries to be maintained, leaders must have a good system for time management. For example, leaders need to make sure to plan time with their family before they fill their calendar up with various meetings and events. Leaders must establish a day off and guard it as well as possible. Leaders might need to set office hours and establish a system by which people can contact them. In essence, leaders must establish boundaries and maintain those boundaries. Failure to do so will result in a leader living his life at the whims of others rather than with distinct and set purpose.

Triple-Loop Learning

Learning involves the detection and correction of error. The typical response to detecting that something needs to change is to look for another strategy to address the problem. In the context of a church, this usually involves looking for a different program or model. In the context of a church leader, the common approach is to look for new book, tool, and so on, hoping that things will change for the better.

Chris Argyris, a world-renowned expert in organizational learning, referred to this as single-loop learning. In single-loop learning, a person simply follows the rules.[10] A leader experiencing single-loop learning seeks to change his behaviors to improve performance or learn a new skill or institute a new procedure in hopes that things will improve.

A different response, one in which a person questions the goals, values, plans, rules, and so on, subjecting them to critical scrutiny, is called double-loop learning. In contrast to single-loop learning, double-loop learning considers changes to the rules.[11] A leader experiencing double-loop learning looks to see if the "rules" should be changed; he looks to see whether or not his mental models, his philosophies, his paradigms, and so on, are the root cause for his behavior and seeks to adjust accordingly. In double-loop learning, the focus shifts from external to internal; this is where a leader can begin the process of improving his thinking.

Argyris explains the difference between single-loop and double-loop learning.

> *If humans repeatedly act differently from their stated goals, it is important to re-examine the underlying values for a possible mismatch or error. There are a least two ways to correct error. The first way is to change the behavior (for example reduce the back biting and bad mouthing among participants in an organization) this is single-loop learning. The second way is to change the governing values that lead to counterproductive behavior. This is double-loop learning.*[12]

I wrote about double-loop learning in my book, *Realign*. I did not, however, address triple-loop learning because I was unaware of it at the time. But having come in contact with the concept, I wanted to share it with you.

Triple-loop learning, a term coined by Richard Foster, is less common than double-loop learning. But I believe it makes a valuable contribution to understanding the learning process.[13] Triple-loop learning takes the learning experience to a third level where the participant learns about learning. A leader experiencing triple-loop learning will reflect on how he learns in the first place. He doesn't stop with thinking whether or not the rule should change; he goes further and considers how he thinks about rules. In this form of learning, leaders learn a great deal more about themselves by examining their beliefs and values, how they came to those beliefs and values, as well as their perceptions and how they came to obtain their perceptions. Triple-loop learning is learning how to learn.

Following is another way of looking at the differences between single-loop, double-loop, and triple-loop learning:
- In single-loop learning the question is, "Are we doing things right?" The focus is behavior.
- In double-loop learning the question is, "Are we doing the right things?" The focus is belief.
- In triple-loop learning the question is, "How do we decide what is right?" The focus is being.

As leaders who desire to grow, we must move beyond single-loop and even double-loop learning. We must seek to make sure our behaviors are what they should be. We must correct our faulty philosophies and beliefs and paradigms. And while all of that is good and well-intended, a leader also must seek to become the change he wishes to see. This is triple-loop learning.

What a leader does (the acts of a leader) is of great importance, but not nearly as important as what a leader is becoming. What a leader does flows from who and what a leader is. Thus, becoming holds greater preeminence than doing. Learning that involves becoming is of great significance in the growth and development of a leader.

Read

I love to read. Thus, when I saw an article on reading written my Michael Hyatt, the former CEO of Thomas Nelson book publishing, I immediately read it. And I loved it. Hyatt, who is also an avid reader, presented five reasons why people who want to be a better leader should read:[14]

1. Reading makes leaders better thinkers.

Hyatt states, "Reading is one of the most efficient ways to acquire information, and leaders need a lot of general information to keep perspective and seize opportunities."[15] But it is more than just finding ideas and acquiring knowledge. "It actually upgrades our analytical tools, especially our judgment and problem-solving abilities."[16] Research shows that in comparison to those who watch television, readers not only know more, they are also better at deciphering misinformation—a crucial trait for effective leadership. Reading improves a leader's judgment and problem-solving abilities. Reading makes a person smarter.

2. Reading improves leaders' people skills.

People often think of people who like to read as introverts with little or no people skills, who always have their nose in a book. But reading can actually improve a leader's people skills. "Stories give us an opportunity to walk in other people's shoes and see the world through their experiences and with their motivations."[17] Looking at things from different perspectives enables leaders to develop empathy and understanding they might not have otherwise acquired.

3. Reading helps leaders master communication.

Reading expands a leader's vocabulary. Hyatt states, "When we read, especially widely and deeply, we pick up language proficiency that transfers across the board, including speaking and writing."[18] Considering the enormous amount of communication involved in leadership, reading should be a huge part of a leader's life. According to research by Anne Cunningham, reading books, magazines, and other written texts uses double and triple the amount of rare words we might not encounter otherwise.[19]

4. Reading helps leaders relax.

An ongoing challenge with every leader is how to manage stress. Surprisingly, a leader can experience a relief from stress by simply reading. Research shows that even as little as six minutes of reading can be enough to reduce stress levels—lowering heart rates and relieving tension—by more than two-thirds, better than walking, listening to music, or drinking a cup of tea.[20] This information led Dr. David Lewis, a neuropsychologist who conducted the research, to say, "Losing yourself in a book is the ultimate relaxation."[21]

5. Reading keeps leaders young.

Reading also helps keep leaders mentally sharp even as they age. According to Robert Wilson, at Rush University Medical Center in Chicago, reading exercises the brain.[22] This exercise is important to brain health in old age, and can actually ward off dementia in later years.

Thus, it behooves leaders to read. Michael Hyatt states, "If you want to lead, you simply must read. It's one of the surest ways to develop the qualities that will make you stand out and simultaneously equip you to lead as your influence grows."[23]

THE GREATEST ENEMY OF PERSONAL GROWTH

Change almost always involves a level of discomfort (uncertainty and/or awkwardness). This is why change is usually resisted. Leaders who want to expand their leadership capacity should expect to experience a certain level of discomfort. Failure to embrace this discomfort almost always results in a lack of growth.

Hence, the greatest enemy to personal growth is to say no to things or times that cause discomfort, uncertainty, or awkwardness. Church leaders, especially after obtaining a certain amount of success, often succumb to the temptation to keep things as they are, giving in to reluctance to reach for something more. Leaders understand that in order to continue moving forward sacrifices must be made. In order to get to where you know you need to go, discomfort must be embraced.

The key to embracing discomfort is to understand where you are headed. If you encounter discomfort while on the path to where you want to go, then embrace it and keep moving forward. Vision determines the usefulness of working through discomfort, uncertainty, and awkwardness. Ask, "Do I know where I am headed? Am I aligned with my purpose? How might pressing through this season of uncertainty help me move closer to where I am headed? How might this season help me grow?

Seasons of growth are disguised as sacrifice, untested waters, awkward opportunities, and so on. Rather than trying to avoid these times, embrace them. To avoid them would be to miss out on an opportunity for growth, growth that is needed if you are going to get to where you are going.

Thus, such is the life of a leader who enhances growth.

EPILOGUE

Jesus was committed to doing the will of the Father. In John 6:38, Jesus said, "For I have come down from heaven, not to do My own will, but the will of Him who sent Me." This commitment was a denial of all self-seeking and self-glorification. That Jesus kept His commitment is seen in His temptation in the wilderness, His prayer in the garden, and His death on the cross.

Likewise, our commitment to doing the will of the Father involves a denial of self. Jesus said, "If anyone desires to come after Me, let him deny himself, and take up his cross, and follow Me" (Matthew 16:24).

G. D. Watson (1845–1924), a Wesleyan Methodist minister, evangelist, and author, describes this committed life in his devotional, "Others May, You Cannot":[24]

> *If God has called you to be really like Jesus, He will draw you into a life of crucifixion and humility, and put upon you such demands of obedience, that you will not be able to follow other people, or measure yourself by other Christians, and in many ways He will seem to let other good people do things which He will not let you do.*
>
> *Other Christians and ministers who seem very religious and useful, may push themselves, pull wires, and work schemes to carry out their plans, but you cannot do it; and if you attempt it, you will meet with such failure and rebuke from the Lord as to make you sorely penitent.*
>
> *Others may boast of themselves, of their work, of their success, of their writings, but the Holy Spirit will not allow you to do any such thing, and if you begin it, He will lead you into some deep mortification that will make you despise yourself and all your good works.*

Others may be allowed to succeed in making money, or may have a legacy left to them, but it is likely God will keep you poor, because He wants you to have something far better than gold, namely, a helpless dependence on Him, that He may have the privilege of supplying your needs day by day out of an unseen treasury.

The Lord may let others be honored and put forward, and keep you hidden in obscurity, because He wants you to produce some choice, fragrant fruit for His coming glory, which can only be produced in the shade. He may let others be great, but keep you small. He may let others do a work for Him and get the credit for it, but He will make you work and toil on without knowing how much you are doing; and then to make your work still more precious, He may let others get the credit for the work which you have done, and thus make your reward ten times greater when Jesus comes.

The Holy Spirit will put a strict watch over you, with a jealous love, and will rebuke you for little words and feelings, or for wasting your time, which other Christians never seem distressed over. So make up your mind that God is an infinite Sovereign, and has a right to do as He pleases with His own. He may not explain to you a thousand things which puzzle your reason in His dealings with you, but if you absolutely sell yourself to be His love slave, He will wrap you up in a jealous love, and bestow upon you many blessings which come only to those who are in the inner circle.

Settle it forever, then, that you are to deal directly with the Holy Spirit, and that He is to have the privilege of tying your tongue, or chaining your hand, or closing your eyes, in ways that He does not seem to use with others. Now when you are so possessed with the loving God that you are, in your secret heart, pleased and delighted over this peculiar, personal, private, jealous guardianship and management of the Holy Spirit over your life, you will have found the vestibule of Heaven.

CONCLUSION

Jesus said, "And I, if I be lifted up from the earth, will draw all men unto me. This he said, signifying what death he should die" (John 12:32–33, KJV). He was not speaking of praise and worship when He spoke of being lifted up. He was speaking of His death—the ultimate denial of self.

Thus, in conclusion, I pray, "May we as church leaders live a life pleasing to Him. May our lives showcase the power of the Cross. Through denial of self and following Him, may others see Christ in us, may we help others experience growth, may we help others become equipped to do ministry, and may many others be drawn unto Him. Amen."

BIBLIOGRAPHY

Allen, Roland. *Missionary Methods: St. Paul's or Ours?* GLH Publishing, 2011. Kindle.

Argyris, Chris. "Chris the Theories of Action, Double-Loop Learning, and Organizational Learning." http://infed.org/mobi/chris-argyris-theories-of-action-double-loop-learning-and-organizational-learning/ (accessed May 15, 2015).

———. "Initiating Change that Preserves." *Journal of Public Administration Research and Theory* 3, (1994): 343-355.

Barclay, William. *The Daily Study Bible: James.* Louisville, KY: Westminster John Knox Press, 1976.

Barna Group. "Americans Divided on the Importance of Church." March 25, 2014. https://www.barna.org/barna-update/culture/661-americans-divided-on-the-importance-of-church#.VPiJnFPF920

Barna, George. *Marketing the Church: What They Never Taught You about Church Growth.* Colorado Springs, CO: Navpress, 1991.

Bass, Bernard M. *Transformational Leadership: Industrial, Military, and Educational Impact.* Mahwah, NJ: Erlbaum, 1998.

Black, J. Stewart, Allen J. Morrison, and Hal B. Gregersen. *Global Explorers: The Next Generation of Leaders.* New York: Routledge, 1999.

Blackaby, Henry and Richard. *Spiritual Leadership: Moving People on to God's Agenda.* Nashville, TN: Bradman & Holman Publishers, 2001.

Block, Peter. *The Flawless Consulting Fieldbook and Companion: A Guide to Understanding Your Expertise.* San Francisco: Jossey-Bass Pfeiffer, 2001.

Caton, Steve. "Ephesians 4 in Practice: How to Equip Disciples for Ministry." Church Community Builder. http://www.churchcommunitybuilder.com/wp-ccb/wp-content/uploads/Eph-4-in-practice.pdf (accessed May 5, 2015).

———. "How Equipping the Saints Helps You Get Unstuck." Tony Morgan Live. November 25, 2014. http://tonymorganlive.com/2014/11/25/equipping-saints-helps-get-unstuck/

Chaves, Mark and Shawna L. Anderson. "Changing American Congregations: Findings from the Third Wave of the National Congregations Study." *Journal for the Scientific Study of Religion* 53, (2014): 676–686.

Christianity Today, "Willow Creek Repents?: Why the Most Influential Church in America Now Says We Made a Mistake." May 18, 2007. http://www.outofur.com/archives/2007/10/willow_creek_re.html

Collins, Jim C. *Good to Great: Why Some Companies Make the Leap and Others Don't*. New York: Harper Business, 2001.

Copenhaver, Martin B. *Jesus Is the Question: The 307 Questions Jesus Asked and the 3 He Answered*. Nashville, TN: Abingdon Press, 2014.

Cunningham, Anne E. "What Reading Does for the Mind," *Journal of Direct Instruction* 1, no. 2 (2001): 137–149. http://www.csun.edu/~krowlands/Content/Academic_Resources/Reading/Useful%20Articles/Cunningham-What%20Reading%20Does%20for%20the%20Mind.pdf

Curtiss, James. "20 Mantras Great Leaders Live By Every Day." *HubSpot Blogs*. January 10, 2015. http://blog.hubspot.com/marketing/leadership-mantras?utm_content=15536356&utm_medium=email&utm_source=hs_email&utm_campaign=blog-rss-emails&success=true

Dunlap, David. "The Myth of 'Growth' in the Church Movement." *Grace Family Journal*. http://www.gracebiblestudies.org/resources/web/www.duluthbible.org/g_f_j/TheMythofGrowth.htm (accessed April 4, 2015).

Edmondson, Ron. "10 Indications a Church Is Making Disciples." July 22, 2014. http://www.ronedmondson.com/2014/07/10-indications-a-church-is-making-disciples.html

———. "12 Leadership Principles of Jesus that Inspire Me." June 19, 2013. http://www.ronedmondson.com/2013/06/12-leadership-principles-of-jesus.html

———. "5 Principles of Making Disciples and Enabling Spiritual Growth." May 19, 2013. http://www.ronedmondson.com/2013/05/5-principles-of-making-disciples-and-enabling-spiritual-growth.html

———. "The Best Leaders Give Their Vision Away." April 27, 2009. http://www.ronedmondson.com/2009/04/leaders-give-your-vision-away.html

BIBLIOGRAPHY

Elmer, Duane. *Cross-Cultural Servanthood: Serving the World in Christlike Humility*. Downers Grove, IL: InterVarsity Press, 2006.

Ephesians 4:12–13 Commentary. Ephesians. http://preceptaustin.org/ephesians_412-13.htm (accessed July 9, 2012).

Ferguson, Dave and Jon. *Exponential*. Zondervan, 2010. Kindle.

Ferguson, Dave. "Explode Those Old Scoreboards." *Christian Standard*. May 10, 2015. http://christianstandard.com/2015/04/explode-those-old-scoreboards/

Foster, Richard. *Innovation: The Attacker's Advantage*. Summit Books, 1986.

Fowler, Susan. "If You Are Holding People Accountable, Something Is Wrong (And it isn't what you think)." *Blanchard LeaderChat*. October 7, 2013. http://leaderchat.org/2013/10/07/if-you-are-holding-people-accountable-something-is-wrong-and-it-isnt-what-you-think/

———. "What Maslow's Hierarchy Won't Tell You About Motivation." *Harvard Business Review*. November 26, 2014. https://hbr.org/2014/11/what-maslows-hierarchy-wont-tell-you-about-motivation

Getz, Gene A. *Sharpening the Focus of the Church*. Wheaton, IL: Victor Books, 1984.

Giselbach, Ben. "Why Your Church Isn't Growing Spiritually." *Plain Simple Faith*. July 16, 2013. http://www.plainsimplefaith.com/2013/07/why-your-church-isnt-growing-spiritually/

Goodstein, Laurie. "Percentage of Protestant Americans Is in Steep Decline, Study Finds." *New York Times*. October 9, 2012. http://www.nytimes.com/2012/10/10/us/study-finds-that-percentage-of-protestant-americans-is-declining.html?_r=0

Greenleaf, Robert K. *The Servant as Leader*. Indianapolis: The Robert K. Greenleaf Center.

Grossman, Cathy Lynn. "Christians Drop, 'Nones' Soar in New Religion Portrait Religion." *USA Today*. May 12, 2015. http://www.usatoday.com/story/news/nation/2015/05/12/christians-drop-nones-soar-in-new-religion-portrait/27159533/

Hartford Institute for Religion Research. "Fast Facts about American Religion." http://hirr.hartsem.edu/research/fastfacts/fast_facts.html (accessed May 4, 2015).

Hyatt, Michael. "5 Ways Reading Makes You a Better Leader: The Science behind Reading and Influence." http://michaelhyatt.com/science-readers-leaders.html#more-29866 (accessed May 18, 2015).

Keller, Timothy. *The Freedom of Self-Forgetfulness*. 2012. Kindle

Krejcir, Richard J. "Focusing on Our Own Will and Desires over the Mission of the Church." http://www.churchleadership.org/apps/articles/default.asp?articleid=42260&columnid=4545 (accessed April 15, 2015).

———. "Pastor and Elders Refusing to Adhere to the Purpose of the Church." http://www.churchleadership.org/apps/articles/default.asp?articleid=42261&columnid=4545 (accessed April 10, 2015).

———. "Setting Boundaries as Pastors." Church Leadership. http://www.churchleadership.org/apps/articles/default.asp?articleid=42891&columnid=4607 (accessed May 12, 2015).

———. "Spiritual Maturity and its Importance." http://www.churchleadership.org/apps/articles/default.asp?articleid=44952&columnid=4545 (accessed March 28, 2015).

———. "Statistics and Reasons for Church Decline." http://www.churchleadership.org/apps/articles/default.asp?articleid=42346&columnid=4545 (accessed March 28, 2015).

———. "Servant Leadership Principles." Church Leadership. http://www.churchleadership.org/apps/articles/?articleid=41928&columnid=4540 (accessed April 3, 2015).

Laurie, Greg. "4 Dangerous Church Growth Myths." Church Leaders. http://www.churchleaders.com/pastors/pastor-articles/164991-greg-laurie-4-dangerous-church-growth-myths.html (accessed April 10, 2015).

Leavitt, H. J. "Why Hierarchies Thrive," *Harvard Business Journal* (2003): 96–102.

Lee-Thorp, Karen. *How to Ask Great Questions*. Colorado Springs, CO: NavPress, 1998.

Lipka, Michael. "What Surveys Say about Worship Attendance—and Why Some Stay Home." Pew Research Center. September 13, 2013. http://www.pewresearch.org/fact-tank/2013/09/13/what-surveys-say-about-worship-attendance-and-why-some-stay-home/

London Jr., H. B. *Pastors at Greater Risk*. Ventura, CA: Regal Books, 2003.

BIBLIOGRAPHY

Maranatha Life. "Statistics about Pastors." Maranatha Life's Life-Line for Pastors. http://maranathalife.com/lifeline/stats.html (accessed June 30, 2012).

Merriam-Webster Dictionary. "Hoopla." http://www.merriam-webster.com/dictionary/hoopla (accessed May 3, 2015).

Michalko, Michael. *Cracking Creativity: The Secrets of Creative Genius.* Berkeley, CA: Ten Speed Press, 2001.

Mind Tools. "5 Whys: Getting to the Root of a Problem Quickly." http://www.mindtools.com/pages/article/newTMC_5W.htm (accessed April 24, 2015).

Mintzberg, Henry, Joseph Lampel, and Bruce Ahlstrand. *Strategy Safari: A Guided Tour through the Wilds of Strategic Management.* New York: Free Press, 2005.

Morgan, G. Campbell. *The Gospel According to Mark.* Oliphants, London, 1956.

Morgan, Garth. *Images of Organization* 2nd ed. Thousand Oaks, CA: Sage Publications, 2006.

Morgan, Tony. "You Fail When You Program Instead of Personalize Leadership Development." Tony Morgan Live. April 22, 2015. http://tonymorganlive.com/2015/04/22/surefire-ways-fail-developing-leaders-part-2/

———. *Big Churches Getting Bigger.* 2012. Kindle.

Myatt, Mike. "10 Reasons Your Top Talent Will Leave You." *Forbes.* December 13, 2012. http://www.forbes.com/sites/mikemyatt/2012/12/13/10-reasons-your-top-talent-will-leave-you/

Nadler, David A. and Michael L. Tushman. *Competing by Design: The Power of Organizational Architecture.* New York: Oxford University Press, 1997.

Nieuwhof, Carey. "10 Very Possible Reasons Your Church Isn't Growing." January 31, 2014. http://careynieuwhof.com/2014/01/10-very-possible-reasons-your-church-isnt-growing/

Northouse, Peter G. *Leadership: Theory and Practice* 4th ed. Thousand Oaks: Sage Publications, 2007.

Olson, David T. "The American Church in Crisis." *Ministry Today.* http://ministrytodaymag.com/index.php/features/17090-the-american-church-in-crisis#sthash.KS6AJtTw.dpuf (accessed May 3, 2015).

Pew Research Center. "America's Changing Religious Landscape." May 12, 2015. http://www.pewforum.org/2015/05/12/americas-changing-religious-landscape/

Pojasek, Robert B. "Asking 'Why' Five Times." *Environmental Quality Management* 10, no. 1 (2000): 79–84.

Press, Harvard Business School, ed. *Harvard Business Review on Becoming a High Performance Manager.* Boston, MA: Harvard Business Press, 2002.

Rainer, Thom S. "One Key Reason Most Churches Do Not Exceed 350 in Average Attendance." Thom S. Rainer. March 25, 2015. http://thomrainer.com/2015/03/25/one-key-reason-churches-exceed-350-average-attendance/

———. "Eleven Observations about Church Transfer Growth." August 9, 2014. http://thomrainer.com/2014/08/09/eleven-observations-church-transfer-growth/

Roberts, Evan. "A Message to the Church," *The Homiletic Review* 49 (1905).

Rockwell, Dan. "How to Motivate Others to Commit." *Leadership Freak.* June 30, 2014. https://leadershipfreak.wordpress.com/2014/06/30/how-to-motivate-others-to-commit/

———. "One Simple Habit that Elevates Leaders." *Leadership Freak.* September 6, 2014. http://leadershipfreak.wordpress.com/2014/09/06/one-simple-habit-that-elevates-leaders/

Salmi, Jamil. "The Growing Accountability Agenda in Tertiary Education: Progress or Mixed Blessing?" *Education Working Paper Series.* January 16, 2009. https://openknowledge.worldbank.org/bitstream/handle/10986/18547/477600EWPS0160Box338865B01PUBLIC1.pdf?sequence=1

Scazzero, Pete. "Characteristics of the Emotionally Unhealthy Leader." Emotionally Healthy Spirituality. March 17, 2015. http://www.emotionallyhealthy.org/characteristics-of-the-emotionally-unhealthy-leader/

———. "How Healthy Is Your Practice of Culture and Team Building?" *Emotionally Healthy Spirituality.* January 29, 2015. http://www.emotionallyhealthy.org/how-healthy-is-your-practice-of-culture-and-team-building/

Shattuck, Kelly. "The American Church in Crisis." *Church Leaders.* http://www.churchleaders.com/outreach-missions/outreach-missions-articles/138908-the-american-church-in-crisis.html (accessed April 29, 2015).

BIBLIOGRAPHY

Sidey, Ken. "Church Growth Fine Tunes Its Formula." *Christianity Today* (1991): 44–47.

Stedman, Ray. "Ephesians 4:12-13 Commentary." http://preceptaustin.org/ephesians_412-13.htm (accessed July 10, 2012).

———. "Jeremiah: A Profile of Courage." Blue Letter Bible. http://www.blueletterbible.org/Comm/stedman_ray/Adv_Jer/Adv_Jer.cfm?a=760018 (accessed April 15, 2015).

Stone, A. Gregory and Kathleen Patterson. "The History of Leadership Focus," *Leadership Research Round Table*. August 2005, https://www.regent.edu/acad/global/publications/sl_proceedings/2005/stone_history.pdf

Stone, Gregory, Robert F. Russell, and Kathleen Patterson. "Transformational versus Servant Leadership: A Difference in Leader Focus," *The Leadership and Organizational Development Journal* 25, no. 4 (2004): 349–364.

Stott, John R. W. *God's New Society: The Message of Ephesians*. Downers Grove, IL: InterVarsity Press, 1979.

The Telegraph, "Reading Can Help Reduce Stress." *The Telegraph*. March 30, 2009. http://www.telegraph.co.uk/news/health/news/5070874/Reading-can-help-reduce-stress.html

Tidal, Derek. "Leaders as Servants: A Resolution of the Tensions," *Evangelical Review of Theology* 36, no. 1 (2012): 31–47.

Unseminary. "How Global Consumer Trends Are Impacting the Church." http://www.unseminary.com/how-global-consumer-trends-are-impacting-your-church-infographic/ (accessed May 10, 2015).

Van der Heyden, Ludo, et al. "Fair Process: Striving for Justice in Family Business," *Family Business Review* 18, no. 1 (2005): 1–21.

VanGoethem, Jeffery. "A Theory of Church Growth." Scofield. http://www.scofield.org/index.php?option=com_content&view=article&id=242%3Aa-theory-of-church-growth&catid=54%3Apastoral-articles&Itemid=289 (accessed April 10, 2015).

Watson, G. D. "Others May, You Cannot." *oChristian*. http://articles.ochristian.com/article14043.shtml (accessed April 28, 2015).

Wilkes, C. Gene. *Jesus on Leadership*. Carol Stream, IL: Tyndale House Publishers, 1998.

Wilson, Robert S., Patricia A. Boyle, and Lei Yu. "Life-Span Cognitive Activity, Neuropathologic Burden, and Cognitive Aging." *Neurology* 81, no. 4 (2013): 314–321.

Winston, Bruce, and Kathleen Patterson, "An Integrative Definition of Leadership," *International Journal of Leadership Studies* 1, no. 2 (2006).

Young, Simeon. Personal Conversation. April 19, 2015.

ENDNOTES

CHAPTER ONE: OVERCOMING THE OSTRICH EFFECT

[1] George Barna, *Marketing the Church*, (Colorado Springs, CO: Navpress, 1990).

[2] Hartford Institute for Religion Research, "Fast Facts about American Religion," http://hirr.hartsem.edu/research/fastfacts/fast_facts.html (accessed May 4, 2015).

[3] Ibid.

[4] Mark Chaves and Shawna L. Anderson, "Changing American Congregations: Findings from the Third Wave of the National Congregations Study," *Journal for the Scientific Study of Religion*, 53 (2014): 676–686.

[5] Barna Group, "Americans Divided on the Importance of Church," March 25, 2014, https://www.barna.org/barna-update/culture/661-americans-divided-on-the-importance-of-church#.VPiJnFPF920

[6] Michael Lipka, "What Surveys Say about Worship Attendance—and Why Some Stay Home," Pew Research Center, September 13, 2013, http://www.pewresearch.org/fact-tank/2013/09/13/what-surveys-say-about-worship-attendance-and-why-some-stay-home/

[7] Cathy Lynn Grossman, "Christians Drop, 'Nones' Soar in New Religion Portrait Religion," *USA Today*, May 12, 2015, http://www.usatoday.com/story/news/nation/2015/05/12/christians-drop-nones-soar-in-new-religion-portrait/27159533/

[8] Laurie Goodstein, "Percentage of Protestant Americans Is in Steep Decline, Study Finds," *New York Times*, October 9, 2012, http://www.nytimes.com/2012/10/10/us/study-finds-that-percentage-of-protestant-americans-is-declining.html?_r=0

[9] Ibid.

[10] Cathy Lynn Grossman, "Christians Drop, 'Nones' Soar in New Religion Portrait Religion."

[11] Pew Research Center, "America's Changing Religious Landscape."

[12] Barna Group, "Americans Divided on the Importance of Church."

[13] Hartford Institute for Religion Research, "Fast Facts about American Religion."

[14] Thom S. Rainer, "One Key Reason Most Churches Do Not Exceed 350 in Average Attendance," Thom S. Rainer, March 25, 2015, http://thomrainer.com/2015/03/25/one-key-reason-churches-exceed-350-average-attendance/

[15] Ibid.

LEADING GROWTH

[16] Hartford Institute for Religion Research, "Fast Facts about American Religion."

[17] David Dunlap, "The Myth of 'Growth' in the Church Growth Movement," *Grace Family Journal*, http://www.gracebiblestudies.org/resources/web/www.duluthbible.org/g_f_j/TheMythofGrowth.htm (accessed April 4, 2015).

[18] Ibid.

[19] Ibid.

[20] Jeffery VanGoethem, "A Theory of Church Growth," *Scofield*, http://www.scofield.org/index.php?option=com_content&view=article&id=242%3Aa-theory-of-church-growth&catid=54%3Apastoral-articles&Itemid=289 (accessed April 20, 2015).

[21] David T. Olson, "The American Church in Crisis," *Ministry Today*, http://ministrytodaymag.com/index.php/features/17090-the-american-church-in-crisis#sthash.KS6AJtTw.dpuf

CHAPTER TWO: PEOPLE ARE NOT GROWING

[1] Barna Group, "Americans Divided on the Importance of Church," March 25, 2014, https://www.barna.org/barna-update/culture/661-americans-divided-on-the-importance-of-church#.VPiJnFPF920

[2] Ibid.

[3] Richard J. Krejcir, "Statistics and Reasons for Church Decline," http://www.churchleadership.org/apps/articles/default.asp?articleid=42346&columnid=4545 (accessed March 28, 2015).

[4] Ibid.

[5] Ibid.

[6] Kelly Shattuck, "The American Church in Crisis," *Church Leaders*, http://www.churchleaders.com/outreach-missions/outreach-missions-articles/138908-the-american-church-in-crisis.html (accessed April 29, 2015).

[7] Ibid.

[8] Ibid.

[9] Barna Group, "Americans Divided on the Importance of Church."

[10] Ibid.

[11] Richard J. Krejcir, "Spiritual Maturity and Its Importance," http://www.churchleadership.org/apps/articles/default.asp?articleid=44952&columnid=4545 (accessed March 28, 2015).

ENDNOTES

[12] Richard J. Krejcir, "Pastor and Elders Refusing to Adhere to the Purpose of the Church," http://www.churchleadership.org/apps/articles/default.

[13] Ibid.

[14] Jeffery VanGoethem, "A Theory of Church Growth," *Scofield*, http://www.scofield.org/index.php?option=com_content&view=a rticle&id=242%3Aa-theory-of-church-growth&catid=54%3Apastoral-articles&Itemid=289 (accessed April 10, 2015).

[15] G. Campbell Morgan, *The Gospel According to Mark* (Oliphants, London, 1956), 177.

[16] Thom Rainer, "Eleven Observations about Church Transfer Growth," August 9, 2014, http://thomrainer.com/2014/08/09/eleven-observations-church-transfer-growth/

[17] Greg Laurie, "4 Dangerous Church Growth Myths," *Church Leaders*, http://www.churchleaders.com/pastors/pastor-articles/164991-greg-laurie-4-dangerous-church-growth-myths.html (accessed April 10, 2015).

[18] Ibid.

[19] Ibid.

[20] Ibid.

[21] Ibid.

[22] Ken Sidey, "Church Growth Fine Tunes Its Formula," *Christianity Today* (June 24, 1991), 46.

[23] David Dunlap, "The Myth of 'Growth' in the Church Movement," *Grace Family Journal*, http://www.gracebiblestudies.org/resources/web/www.duluthbible.org/g_f_j/TheMythofGrowth.htm (accessed April 4, 2015).

[24] Christianity Today. "Willow Creek Repents?: Why the Most Influential Church in America Now Says We Made a Mistake," *Christianity Today*, http://www.outofur.com/archives/2007/10/willow_creek_re.html (accessed June 10, 2012).

[25] Ibid.

[26] Greg Laurie, "4 Dangerous Church Growth Myths."

[27] Ibid.

[28] Ibid.

CHAPTER THREE: WHY DO YOU WANT TO GROW?

[1] Dan Rockwell, One Simple Habit that Elevates Leaders," *Leadership Freak*, September 6, 2014, http://leadershipfreak.wordpress.com/2014/09/06/one-simple-habit-that-elevates-leaders/

[2] Ibid.

[3] Ibid.

[4] Ibid.

[5] Mind Tools, "5 Whys: Getting to the Root of a Problem Quickly," http://www.mindtools.com/pages/article/newTMC_5W.htm (accessed April 24, 2015).

[6] Robert B. Pojasek, "Asking 'Why' Five Times," *Environmental Quality Management* 10 no. 1, (2000): 79–84.

[7] Matthew 20:25–28.

[8] Philippians 2:3–4.

[9] I Peter 5:2–3.

[10] Timothy Keller, *The Freedom of Self-Forgetfulness* (Kindle: 2012), 143–147.

[11] Ibid. 156.

[12] Ibid. 269–273.

[13] Ibid. 290–291.

[14] Ibid. 290–295.

[15] Ray Stedman, "Jeremiah: A Profile of Courage," *Blue Letter Bible*, http://www.blueletterbible.org/Comm/stedman_ray/Adv_Jer/Adv_Jer.cfm?a=760018 (accessed April 15, 2015).

[16] Romans 12:3.

[17] Jim C. Collins, *Good to Great: Why Some Companies Make the Leap and Others Don't.* (New York: Harper Business, 2001).

[18] Ibid. 28.

[19] Matthew 20:25–28.

[20] Jeremiah 17:9.

CHAPTER FOUR: ARE YOU ALIGNED WITH GOD'S PLAN?

[1] Roland B. Allen, *Missionary Methods: St. Paul's or Ours?* (Kindle: GLH Publishing, 2011), 28–29.

[2] Ephesians 4:12–13 Commentary. *Ephesians*, http://preceptaustin.org/ephesians_412-13.htm. (accessed July 9, 2012).

ENDNOTES

[3] Ibid.

[4] Ibid.

[5] Ray Stedman, "Ephesians 4:12–13 Commentary," http://preceptaustin.org/ephesians_412-13.htm (accessed July 10, 2012).

[6] John R. W. Stott. *God's New Society: The Message of Ephesians* (Downers Grove, IL: Inter-Varsity Press, 1979), 167.

[7] Ben Giselbach, "Why Your Church Isn't Growing Spiritually," *Plain Simple Faith*, July 16, 2013, http://www.plainsimplefaith.com/2013/07/why-your-church-isnt-growing-spiritually/

[8] Simeon Young, Personal Conversation, April 19, 2015.

[9] William Barclay, *The Daily Study Bible: James* (Louisville, KY: Westminster John Know Press, 1976).

[10] Richard J. Krejcir, "Focusing on Our Own Will and Desires over the Mission of the Church," http://www.churchleadership.org/apps/articles/default.asp?articleid=42260&columnid=4545 (accessed April 15, 2015).

[11] William Barclay, *The Daily Study Bible: James*.

CHAPTER FIVE: MEASURING GROWTH

[1] Dave Ferguson, "Explode Those Old Scoreboards," *Christian Standard*, May 10, 2015, http://christianstandard.com/2015/04/explode-those-old-scoreboards/

[2] Ibid.

[3] Ibid.

[4] Ibid.

[5] Steve Caton, "Ephesians 4 in Practice: How to Equip Disciples for Ministry," *Church Community Builder*, http://www.churchcommunitybuilder.com/wp-ccb/wp-content/uploads/Eph-4-in-practice.pdf (accessed May 5, 2015).

[6] Ibid.

[7] Dave Ferguson and Jon Ferguson, *Exponential* (Kindle: Zondervan, 2010), 79.

[8] Ron Edmondson, "10 Indications a Church Is Making Disciples," *Ron Edmondson*, July 22, 2014, http://www.ronedmondson.com/2014/07/10-indications-a-church-is-making-disciples.html

[9] Ibid.

[10] Steve Caton, "Ephesians 4 in Practice: How to Equip Disciples for Ministry."

[11] Ibid.

[12] Ibid.

[13] Ron Edmondson, "10 Indications a Church Is Making Disciples."

[14] Pete Scazzero, "How Healthy Is Your Practice of Culture and Team Building?" *Emotionally Healthy Spirituality*, January 29, 2015, http://www.emotionallyhealthy.org/how-healthy-is-your-practice-of-culture-and-team-building/

CHAPTER SIX: LEADERSHIP STYLES

[1] Carey Nieuwhof, "10 Very Possible Reasons Your Church Isn't Growing," January 31, 2014, http://careynieuwhof.com/2014/01/10-very-possible-reasons-your-church-isnt-growing/

[2] Bruce Winston and Kathleen Patterson, "An Integrative Definition of Leadership," *International Journal of Leadership Studies* 1, no. 2 (2006): 7.

[3] Henry Blackaby and Richard Blackaby, *Spiritual Leadership: Moving People on to God's Agenda* (Nashville, TN: Bradman & Holman Publishers, 2001).

[4] Peter G. Northouse, *Leadership: Theory and Practice* 4th ed. (Thousand Oaks: Sage Publications, 2007), 3.

[5] Steve Caton, "How Equipping the Saints Helps You Get Unstuck," *Tony Morgan Live*, November 25, 2014, http://tonymorganlive.com/2014/11/25/equipping-saints-helps-get-unstuck/

[6] Bruce Winston and Kathleen Patterson, "An Integrative Definition of Leadership."

CHAPTER SEVEN: WHAT'S ALL THE HOOPLA ABOUT SERVANT LEADERSHIP?

[1] Richard Krejcir, "Servant Leadership Principles," *Church Leadership*, http://www.churchleadership.org/apps/articles/?articleid=41928&columnid=4540 (accessed April 3, 2015).

[2] Ibid.

[3] *Merriam-Webster Dictionary*, "Hoopla," http://www.merriam-webster.com/dictionary/hoopla (accessed May 3, 2015).

ENDNOTES

[4] Robert K. Greenleaf, *The Servant as Leader*. (Indianapolis: The Robert K. Greenleaf Center).

[5] Ibid.

[6] Ibid.

[7] A. Gregory Stone and Kathleen Patterson, "The History of Leadership Focus," Leadership Research Round Table, August 2005, https://www.regent.edu/acad/global/publications/sl_proceedings/2005/stone_history.pdf

[8] Derek Tidal, "Leaders as Servants: A Resolution of the Tensions," *Evangelical Review of Theology* 36, no. 1 (2012), 31.

[9] Ibid. 31–47.

[10] Ibid. 36.

[11] Ibid. 35.

[12] Ibid. 35.

[13] Ibid. 31.

[14] Ibid. 31–32.

[15] Ibid. 32.

[16] Ibid. 32.

[17] Ibid. 32.

[18] Ibid. 33.

[19] Ibid. 33.

[20] Ibid. 45.

[21] Ibid. 46.

[22] Ibid. 46.

[23] Ibid. 46.

[24] Duane Elmer, *Cross-Cultural Servanthood: Serving the World in Christlike Humility* (Downers Grove, IL: InterVarsity Press, 2006), 156.

[25] Gregory Stone, Robert F. Russell, and Kathleen Patterson, "Transformational versus Servant Leadership: A Difference in Leader Focus," *The Leadership & Organizational Development Journal* 25, no. 24 (2004): 354.

[26] Bernard M. Bass. *Transformational Leadership: Industrial, Military, and Educational Impact* (Mahwah, NJ: Erlbaum, 1998), 26.

CHAPTER EIGHT: GROWTH ACTIVITIES

[1] Harvard Business Review, *Becoming a High-Performance Manager* (Harvard Business School Press, 2002), 39–66.

[2] Ron Edmondson, "12 Leadership Principles of Jesus that Inspire Me," June 19, 2013, http://www.ronedmondson.com/2013/06/12-leadership-principles-of-jesus.html

[3] James Curtiss, "20 Mantras Great Leaders Live By Every Day," *HobSpot Blogs*, January 10, 2015, http://blog.hubspot.com/marketing/leadership-mantras?utm_content=15536356&utm_medium=email&utm_source=hs_email&utm_campaign=blog-rss-emails&success=true

[4] Gene A. Getz, *Sharpening the Focus of the Church* (Wheaton, IL: Victor Books, 1984), 56.

[5] Martin B. Copenhaver, *Jesus is the Question: The 307 Questions Jesus Asked and the 3 He Answered* (Nashville, TN: Abingdon Press, 2014).

[6] Karen Lee-Thorp, *How to Ask Great Questions* (Colorado Springs, CO: NavPress, 1998), 5.

[7] Dan Rockwell, "How to Motivate Others to Commit," *Leadership Freak*, June 30, 2014, https://leadershipfreak.wordpress.com/2014/06/30/how-to-motivate-others-to-commit/

[8] Susan Fowler, "What Maslow's Hierarchy Won't Tell You About Motivation," *Harvard Business Review*, November 26, 2014, https://hbr.org/2014/11/what-maslows-hierarchy-wont-tell-you-about-motivation

[9] Ibid.

[10] Ibid.

[11] Ibid.

[12] Dan Rockwell, "How to Motivate Others to Commit," *Leadership Freak*, June 30, 2014, https://leadershipfreak.wordpress.com/2014/06/30/how-to-motivate-others-to-commit/

[13] J. Stewart Black, Allen J. Morrison, and Hal B. Gregersen, *Global Explorers: The Next Generation of Leaders* (New York: Routledge, 1999), 112.

[14] Michael Michalko. Cracking Creativity: *The Secrets of Creative Genius* (Berkeley, CA: Ten Speed Press, 2001), 259.

[15] Tony Morgan, *Big Churches Getting Bigger* (Kindle, 2012), 85–86.

[16] C. Gene Wilkes, *Jesus on Leadership* (Carol Stream, IL: Tyndale House Publishers, 1998).

[17] Ibid. 191.

ENDNOTES

[18] Ibid. 191.

[19] Ibid. 193.

[20] Garth Morgan, *Images of Organization* 2nd ed. (Thousand Oaks, CA: Sage Publications, 2006), 69.

CHAPTER NINE: IS ACCOUNTABILITY EFFECTIVE?

[1] Susan Fowler, "If You Are Holding People Accountable, Something Is Wrong (And it isn't what you think)," Blanchard LeaderChat, October 7, 2013 http://leaderchat.org/2013/10/07/if-you-are-holding-people-accountable-something-is-wrong-and-it-isnt-what-you-think/

[2] Ibid.

[3] Ibid.

[4] Ludo Van der Heyden, et al., "Fair Process: Striving for Justice in Family Business," *Family Business Review* 18, no. 1 (2005):1–21.

[5] Susan Fowler, "If You Are Holding People Accountable, Something Is Wrong (And it isn't what you think").

[6] Ibid.

[7] Ibid.

[8] Jamil Salmi, "The Growing Accountability Agenda in Tertiary Education: Progress or Mixed Blessing?" *Education Working Paper Series*, January 2009, https://openknowledge.worldbank.org/bitstream/handle/10986/18547/477600EWPS0160Box338865B01PUBLIC1.pdf?sequence=1

CHAPTER TEN: STRATEGIC THINKING FOR GROWTH

[1] Ron Edmondson, "5 Principles of Making Disciples and Enabling Spiritual Growth," May 19, 2013, http://www.ronedmondson.com/2013/05/5-principles-of-making-disciples-and-enabling-spiritual-growth.html

[2] Henry Mintzberg, Bruce Ahlstrand, and Joseph Lampel. *Strategy Safari: A Guided Tour through the Wilds of Strategic Management* (New York: The Free Press, 2005), 9.

[3] Ron Edmondson, "5 Principles of Making Disciples and Enabling Spiritual Growth."

[4] Steve Caton, "Ephesians 4 in Practice: How to Equip Disciples for Ministry," *Church*

Community Builder, http://www.churchcommunitybuilder.com/wp-ccb/wp-content/uploads/Eph-4-in-practice.pdf (accessed May 5, 2015).

[5] Ibid.

[6] Mike Myatt, "10 Reasons Your Top Talent Will Leave You." *Forbes.* December 13, 2012, http://www.forbes.com/sites/mikemyatt/2012/12/13/10-reasons-your-top-talent-will-leave-you/

[7] Ibid.

[8] Ibid.

[9] Ibid.

[10] Tony Morgan, "You Fail When You Program Instead of Personalize Leadership Development," Tony Morgan Live, April 22, 2015, http://tonymorganlive.com/2015/04/22/surefire-ways-fail-developing-leaders-part-2/

[11] Ibid.

[12] Ron Edmondson, "The Best Leaders Give Their Vision Away," April 27, 2009, http://www.ronedmondson.com/2009/04/leaders-give-your-vision-away.html

[13] Evan Roberts, "A Message to the Church," *The Homiletic Review*, 49, (1905), 173.

[14] David A. Nadler, and Michael L. Tushman, *Competing by Design: The Power of Organizational Architecture* (New York: Oxford University Press, 1997), 53.

[15] H. J. Leavitt, "Why Hierarchies Thrive," *Harvard Business Journal*, (2003): 98.

[16] Peter Block, *The Flawless Consulting Fieldbook and Companion: A Guide to Understanding Your Expertise* (San Francisco: Jossey-Bass Pfeiffer, 2001), 342.

[17] Carey Nieuwhof, "Cultural Trends Church Leaders Can't Ignore (But Might)," June 7, 2013, http://careynieuwhof.com/2013/06/12-cultural-trends-church-leaders-cant-ignore-but-might/

[18] Ibid.

[19] Ibid.

[20] Ibid.

[21] Unseminary, "How Global Consumer Trends are Impacting the Church," http://www.unseminary.com/how-global-consumer-trends-are-impacting-your-church-infographic/ (accessed May 10, 2015).

[22] Ibid.

ENDNOTES

CHAPTER ELEVEN: GROW YOURSELF

[1] Richard J. Krejcir, "Setting Boundaries as Pastors," *Church Leadership*, http://www.churchleadership.org/apps/articles/default.asp?articleid=42891&columnid=4607 (accessed May 12, 2015).

[2] Maranatha Life, "Statistics about Pastors," *Maranatha Life's Life-Line for Pastors*, http://maranathalife.com/lifeline/stats.htm (accessed June 30, 2012).

[3] H. B. London Jr., *Pastors at Greater Risk* (Ventura, CA: Regal Books, 2003).

[4] Maranatha Life, "Statistics about Pastors."

[5] Ibid.

[6] Ibid.

[7] Pete Scazzero, "Characteristics of the Emotionally Unhealthy Leader," *Emotionally Healthy Spirituality*, March 17, 2015, http://www.emotionallyhealthy.org/characteristics-of-the-emotionally-unhealthy-leader/

[8] Ibid.

[9] Ibid.

[10] Ibid.

[11] Ibid.

[12] Chris Argyris, "Initiating Change That Preserves," *Journal of Public Administration Research and Theory* 3 (1994): 345.

[13] Richard Foster, *Innovation: the Attacker's Advantage* (Summit Books, 1986).

[14] Michael Hyatt, "5 Ways Reading Makes You a Better Leader: The Science behind Reading and Influence," http://michaelhyatt.com/science-readers-leaders.html#more-29866 (accessed May 18, 2015).

[15] Ibid.

[16] Ibid.

[17] Ibid.

[18] Ibid.

[19] Anne E. Cunningham, "What Reading Does for the Mind," *Journal of Direct Instruction* 1, no. 2 (2001): 137–149, http://www.csun.edu/~krowlands/Content/Academic_Resources/Reading/Useful%20Articles/Cunningham-What%20Reading%20Does%20for%20the%20Mind.pdf

[20] *The Telegraph*, "Reading Can Help Reduce Stress," *The Telegraph*, March 30, 2009, http://www.telegraph.co.uk/news/health/news/5070874/Reading-can-help-reduce-stress.html

[21] Ibid.

[22] Robert S. Wilson, Patricia A. Boyle, and Lei Yu, "Life-Span Cognitive Activity, Neuropathologic Burden, and Cognitive Aging." *Neurology*, 81 (2013).

[23] Michael Hyatt, "5 Ways Reading Makes You a Better Leader: The Science behind Reading and Influence."